2.23 ✓
Ref

How to Complete Your UCAS Application

2023 Entry

Ray Le Tarouilly and UCAS

34th edition

Getting into guides

Getting into Art & Design Courses, 12th edition
Getting into Business & Economics Courses, 14th edition
Getting into Dental School, 12th edition
Getting into Engineering Courses, 6th edition
Getting into Law, 14th edition
Getting into Medical School 2023 Entry, 27th edition
Getting into Oxford and Cambridge 2023 Entry, 25th edition
Getting into Pharmacy and Pharmacology Courses, 2nd edition
Getting into Physiotherapy Courses, 10th edition
Getting into Psychology Courses, 14th edition
Getting into Veterinary School, 12th edition

How to Complete Your UCAS Application 2023 Entry

This 34th edition published in 2022 by Trotman Education, an imprint of Trotman Indigo Publishing Ltd, 21d Charles Street, Bath BA1 1HX

© Trotman Indigo Publishing Ltd 2022

Authors: Ray Le Tarouilly and UCAS

Foreword by Sander Kristel © Sander Kristel

Screenshots from UCAS application system, Figures 3–21 © UCAS. Reproduced with kind permission of UCAS.

British Library Cataloguing in Publication Data
A catalogue record for this book is available from the British Library

ISBN 978 1 912943 66 1

Printed and bound in Gloucester, UK by Severn.

Contents

Foreword

First decision: where to begin?

Congratulations! You've made an important decision to consider your options and potentially apply to a university or college course, or for an apprenticeship. With so many choices to make you might need some help in deciding what is best for you or what and where to study. This book will help you turn that decision into a reality.

We at UCAS believe giving you access to as much information as possible is vital in helping you to make a good decision about your future studies.

The research you do and the advice you get can provide a valuable insight into which method of study or which course is right for you. The UCAS Hub on ucas.com should be your starting point – register now to explore, research and chat to current students. After registration there is no obligation to apply, and you can explore a wide range of options. The UCAS Careers Quiz in the Hub, for instance, has already supported hundreds of thousands of people, just like you, to make their choices.

When you're ready to begin your search for courses or apprenticeships, the UCAS search tool and UCAS' Career Finder are the definitive sources of information on your options. We advise you to look closely at this information, be realistic about entry requirements and, if possible, make a visit to the universities and colleges you're interested in. Remember, you could potentially be spending three or four years there, so it needs to feel like the right place for you.

This guide will tell you what you need to know about applying, and make sure you also head to ucas.com where we've got tips and blogs from students, parents and advisers. Have a look around – and if you have a question that remains unanswered, get in touch.

Best of luck with your research and application!

Sander Kristel
Chief Operating Officer, UCAS

Introduction

This book is intended to be a guide for anyone wanting to gain a place on a UK higher education course. In the 2020/21 application cycle, 749,570 people applied for undergraduate courses, an increase of 2.8% on the previous year. Of these, 562,060 were accepted through UCAS to start an undergraduate course in 2021. All of these students had to complete UCAS applications to try to gain their university or college place.

The job of UCAS

With very few exceptions, every application to a full-time higher education course must be made through UCAS – whether a degree, a course leading to a degree, a Foundation degree, Higher National Diploma (HND) or Diploma of Higher Education (DipHE). UCAS manages and monitors the flow of applications to universities and colleges and their decisions to applicants. UCAS acts as the intermediary between students and their chosen universities and colleges, providing lists of available courses and the means by which prospective students can apply for them.

As well as handling initial applications, UCAS offers Clearing as a way for students to find a place when the summer exam results come out. Find out more about Clearing in Chapter 10.

UCAS offers a lot of help for higher education and apprenticeship applicants on ucas.com, where you can:

- register for the UCAS Hub – allowing you to explore and research your options, and even chat to current students based at universities and colleges around the UK
- take the UCAS Careers Quiz to find your ideal career and see what courses previous students studied to get there
- use the UCAS search tool to research the courses offered by different universities and colleges – using a number of variables, such as qualification (degree, HND, etc.), subject, university or college, or geographical area
- use UCAS' Career Finder to search for apprenticeships, filter by subject area, role type, location and level, and sign up for alerts to keep you posted on the latest opportunities

- find out the entry requirements for courses, including grades and Tariff* points and any additional requirements
- find out more about each course, including its content, teaching methods and method of assessment
- make an application to your chosen university courses
- follow the progress of your application
- find an additional course to apply to if you've used all your choices and you aren't holding any offers (through our Extra* service)
- get information about financing your studies
- go through Clearing* if you have your results but no offers.

* All these terms are explained in the Glossary (see page 171).

Of course, applying through UCAS is no guarantee of a place on a higher education course. Every year, a number of people apply but aren't offered places.

Using this guide

This book is divided into three parts. A brief outline of the content and purpose of each part is given below.

Part I. In the think tank

Before you make a UCAS application, research all your higher education options thoroughly. The first part of this guide gives you a number of ideas about the areas you need to consider carefully before you can be confident of making the right higher education course choices. These six chapters guide you through the decision-making process, helping you to find answers to key questions, such as:

- is higher education the right option for me? (Chapter 1)
- how will a degree or higher diploma fit in with my career plans? (Chapter 2)
- how will I afford it? (Chapter 3)
- how do I choose what and where to study? (Chapters 4 and 5)
- will I meet the entry requirements? (Chapter 6)

You need to be ready to explain and justify your decision. Admissions tutors read your UCAS application and may interview you – they'll want to know why you've applied for a place on their particular course. At the end of most chapters there's a 'Resources' section suggesting points of reference you can access in your school or college library, or your local careers centre. Ask advisers for help in finding the most up-to-date materials.

Part II. The admissions procedure: applications, interviews, offers and beyond

Once you've decided which courses to apply for, Part II provides an overview of the entire admissions procedure. It works through the whole process, answering key questions such as:

- when do I submit my application? (Chapter 7)
- how do universities and colleges communicate their offers to me? (Chapter 7)
- how do I accept or decline offers? (Chapter 7)
- what about non-standard applications? (Chapter 8)
- how can I maximise my chances if I'm called for interview? (Chapter 9)
- what happens on exam results day? (Chapter 10)
- how do I use Clearing? (Chapter 10)

Part III. Your UCAS application

Part III covers the technicalities of filling in and submitting your UCAS application online, taking you through the process step by step and offering helpful advice and tips.

Timetable for advanced-level students

If you stick to the timetable, the whole process of applying to higher education is straightforward. The application timetable below gives you an idea of what to do and when.

Please note: the term advanced-level students doesn't mean simply A level students – it's for all students doing any advanced or level 3 course.

First year of advanced-level course

Autumn term

- Start to explore the range of possible options beyond your advanced-level courses at school or college. (Chapters 1 and 2)
- Consider your GCSE or equivalent qualifications – the range and grades achieved – and review any A level, Scottish Higher, International Baccalaureate (IB), Irish Leaving Certificate (ILC) or BTEC National subjects you're taking. (Chapter 6)
- Will your qualifications help you to achieve your future plans? Discuss this with your careers adviser.

Spring term
- Work through a skills, aptitudes and interests guide like MyUniChoices (www.myunichoices.com) or Morrisby Profile (www. morrisby.com/morrisby-profile), or complete a career development profiling exercise. (Chapter 2)
- Start to research your higher education options in the light of these results. Prepare for and attend a UCAS higher education exhibition. (Chapters 4 and 5)
- Explore the financial implications of attending a higher education course. (Chapter 3)

Summer term
- Prepare for and attend a UCAS exhibition, if you missed out on this in the spring. (Chapters 4 and 5)
- Attend university and college open days.
- Continue to research your higher education options, checking UCAS course requirements and entry profiles.
- Draw up a shortlist of possible universities and/or colleges.
- Make decisions on courses and modules to take next year.
- Arrange to do work experience during the summer. This is important for entry to some courses, for example medicine, those leading to healthcare professions (such as occupational therapy, physiotherapy, radiography and speech therapy), veterinary science and veterinary medicine, social work, the land-based industries and teaching degree courses. (Chapter 2)
- Try to obtain sponsorship for courses – write to possible organisations you have researched. (Chapter 3)
- Start to organise your year out if you plan to take a gap year.
- Gather up material evidence from which to draft a personal statement for your UCAS application. (Chapter 21)
- Research details for sitting the University Clinical Aptitude Test (UCAT), which is required for entry to medicine and dentistry at some universities. You can register from 24 May 2022, book your test between 20 June and midday on 22 September 2022, and take the test between 11 July and 29 September 2022. (Chapter 9)

Summer holidays
- Undertake the work experience you arranged during the summer term. Keep a diary of what you did so that you can refer back to it when you write your personal statement. (Chapter 21)
- Possibly attend a taster course (which can be arranged by many universities). (Chapter 4)

Second year of advanced-level course

Autumn term

- Between 6 September 2022 and the equal-consideration date (which is either 15 October or 25 January depending on your course), submit your completed UCAS application (Chapter 7 and Part III).
- Registration for and booking of the Law National Aptitude Test (LNAT) for September 2023 entry opens on 1 August 2022. Testing starts on 1 September 2022. The standard closing date for booking a test is 15 January 2023, and the last date you can sit the LNAT is 20 January 2023. (NB: Some universities have an earlier closing date. (Chapter 9)
- On 2 November 2022 you can register for the BMAT – BioMedical Admissions Test. Late entry fees apply. (Chapter 9)
- Before 29 September 2022 take the UCAT test if necessary.
- Before 18.00 (UK time) on 15 October, submit your UCAS application for the universities of Oxford and Cambridge. The University of Oxford requires some extra information for some international interviews and for choral or organ awards. (Chapter 8 and Part III)
- Before 18.00 (UK time) on 15 October, submit all UCAS applications for entry to medicine, dentistry, veterinary science and veterinary medicine.

Spring term

- 25 January 2023 at 18.00 (UK time) is the equal-consideration date for UCAS to receive applications for all courses except those with a 15 October deadline. Use the UCAS search tool at www.ucas.com to check your course deadline.
- Apply for bursaries, sponsorship or scholarships as appropriate.
- Prepare for possible interviews with admissions tutors; a mock interview if your school/college offers them is useful at this point.
- If you live in England, Wales and Northern Ireland, you should make your application for financial assessment through the Student Loans Company, whatever your particular circumstances. Applicants from Scotland make their application for financial assessment to the Student Awards Agency for Scotland (SAAS).
- From 23 February 2023, if you used all five choices in your application but aren't holding an offer of a place, you can use the Extra option.

Summer term

- By 18 May 2023, decisions should have been received from all universities and colleges if you applied by 25 January.
- If you receive all your university and college decisions by 18 May, you should reply to any offers by 8 June.
- 30 June 2023 at 18:00 (UK time) is the last date for receipt of applications before Clearing.
- Until 4 July, further applications can be made using UCAS Extra (if you applied for five courses originally and are not holding an offer).

Summer holidays

- 7 July 2022 is IB results day (the date for 2023 is still to be confirmed).
- 18 August 2022 is A level results day (the date for 2023 is still to be confirmed).
- 9 August 2022 is Scottish Highers results day (the date for 2023 is still to be confirmed).
- UCAS Clearing vacancy information is available from 5 July 2023. If you don't get the results you were hoping for, you may need additional support through Clearing to find an alternative higher education option or further information and guidance from your local careers service.
- 21 September 2023 is the last date for Clearing applications.

Part I
In the think tank

1| Is higher education right for you?

Overview of higher education today

Applying for entry to higher education may well be the most important step that you've taken up to now. It's one that will certainly affect the next three or more years of your life and in the long term will affect your career choices and prospects, which in turn will impact on your future lifestyle.

There are plenty of people who can help you choose your higher education course and place of study – your careers adviser, your careers and subject teachers, your present employer and your family and friends. The decision is ultimately yours though, and you'll need to be confident about the suitability of your chosen higher education course.

Every year, people take up places only to find that the course content, teaching style or institution isn't what they expected – and they subsequently leave their courses. The average non-continuation rate during the first year of study on a full-time first degree course is 6.7% for the UK as a whole, but the rate at individual universities and colleges varies considerably (source: Higher Education Statistics Agency).

This can be difficult, not just for the student but also for the university or college, so it is worth taking the time at this stage to make sure that your application choices are right for you.

All about you

Before considering higher education courses have a think about the following questions.

Are you happy to continue in education?

Going on to higher education is a big step to take. Put simply, you've got to be committed and enthusiastic. If you don't enjoy your chosen course, you will find your time in higher education very difficult.

Advanced-level study – for example GCE, A level, Scottish Higher, Irish Leaving Certificate (ILC), International Baccalaureate (IB), BTEC National Award and so on – is an essential preparation for many aspects of higher education, not just in terms of subject-specific knowledge but also in terms of analytical skills. On your higher education course, you'll be further developing your powers of deduction, reasoning, critical analysis and evaluation – just as much as you'll be learning new facts about your chosen subject. Are you ready for this?

There are literally thousands of courses, and many include opportunities for practical learning, work experience and studying abroad. Do you like the sound of this?

Have you seriously explored your aptitudes, interests and career aspirations?

Do you want to learn more because you have strong ability in a particular area and because you find the subject matter interesting? If so, you are in a good starting position and you're likely to enjoy your studies.

Some degree-level courses explore one particular subject area in great depth, with no direct link to employment or a career structure (for example history, anthropology, geography, physics, English, American studies and French). Have you thought about what you'll do once you graduate? How will your degree link with your long-term career plan? (See Chapter 2 for more on this.) A degree may only be a stepping stone to the start of a professional career – once you're in employment, it is often necessary to continue studying to gain professional qualifications. So you'll need commitment to reach your goals.

Some people are influenced by promotional publicity or by the enthusiasm of other people, and don't consider the possible long-term impact of their choice on themselves. You need to think carefully about this. Step back and try a number of aptitude and interest guides that are available online and in careers centres (see the 'Resources' section at the end of Chapter 2).

Are you ready to be a student?

Student life is likely to offer you all of the social and extracurricular opportunities you ever dreamed of. Are you confident you can balance your social life with your studies – especially if you apply for a course with fewer scheduled contact hours, such as English or history? Remember, there's a big change from the guided learning you've experienced at school or college to the self-management of study in higher education.

You'll have to develop your own study skills and become an independent, self-motivated learner. Your subject teachers or tutors can offer helpful guidance on this point.

Don't be surprised if you feel confused and uncertain about applying to courses a long way from home. You're taking an important decision that may result in you striking out on your own, seemingly leaving behind everything you find familiar. It's natural to feel apprehensive about this – many people do experience insecurity and can feel isolated and disorientated at first, but most find they adapt very quickly.

If you're feeling very worried about the prospect of leaving home, talk to a friendly careers adviser, student adviser, personal tutor, or a friend or relative, and focus on the positive aspects of your higher education intentions. It's important to make sure you're clear about your plans and the changes these will mean for your day-to-day life.

Lastly – money. How you're going to finance your higher education course is likely to be a major consideration. You'll need to give careful thought to the financial implications of going through higher education. For example, some people decide to live at home rather than go away in order to save money. Some choose universities and colleges that offer cheaper accommodation. Others look carefully at the scholarships and bursaries on offer at different places. This subject is discussed in depth in Chapter 3.

Chapter summary

The decision to pursue a higher education course isn't one to take lightly. However, if you have read through the questions and points above and still feel confident that higher education is the right choice for you, read on. The rest of Part I will help you focus your research so you can narrow down the huge number of courses on offer to the ones you'll enter on your UCAS application (you can add between one and five courses).

As you work through the following chapters, keep testing yourself by asking the following questions.

- Have I given enough consideration to each point?
- Which resources proved useful in my research?
- Have I talked to people with knowledge or experience in this area?
- Will I feel the same in two or three years?
- Should I do more research?

Essential research

● Talk to subject teachers, tutors or form teachers and careers advisers.

● Check to see whether your local careers service gives information on higher education opportunities on its website.

● Use the timetable on pages 3 to 6 to draw up your own calendar of important dates and deadlines. You will need to make decisions about courses to apply to in the autumn term of 2022, and then you'll need to meet all subsequent UCAS deadlines.

● Register for your UCAS Hub on ucas.com to start your research and chat to current students.

2 | Looking to the future: career routes

Since you'll be committing a lot of time and money to study a higher education course, it's vital to research possible graduate career routes. This is the moment for in-depth careers exploration and planning, looking at where a particular subject area might take you and what previous graduates have gone on to do.

This may seem tricky. How can you possibly know what you want to do in four years' time? How can you narrow down the options when you are having enough trouble just choosing which courses to apply for? Some people, of course, do have firm career ideas. For others, the idea of planning for the future can be difficult – because there's simply too much choice. It may also seem time consuming when you are busy working for exams.

In most cases, investigating possible careers doesn't mean committing yourself to one particular career at this stage. Remember, any decisions you make or ideas you have at this stage aren't set in stone. You can change and adapt your plans as you go. It's good to have some career ideas though, not least because admissions tutors want to see that you're looking ahead, and that you'll be an interested and motivated student with career plans beyond your time at university or college. Plus, thinking about your plans now will prepare you for career-related questions if you're invited to an interview (see Chapter 9).

There are many people who can help you form some ideas about a future career, but ideally your first port of call should be your school or college's careers department or a chat with a careers adviser. Unfortunately, availability varies in different areas, but there are other people you can ask for help, too – like parents, friends, former students from your school or college – and there are useful online tools which your school or college might have. (These are listed at the end of the chapter.)

Developing a career plan

If you already have a career plan

Now's the time to research it in as much depth as possible. Find out which courses are the most relevant and which get you professional accreditation in the career you have chosen (if applicable). For many careers, a degree is only the first step – you'll have to undertake further training, often in employment, in order to qualify (e.g. accountancy and engineering). Also, find out which courses have the best record of placing graduates in their chosen career area. (For more on this, see Chapters 4 and 5.)

If you already know what subject interests you, but you don't know what you want to do next

This is the time to do some broad research. Take a look at a careers directory or website (see the 'Resources' section at the end of this chapter) to find out what's out there, and focus on the jobs that seem to relate to your chosen subject. Research possible progression routes and projected salaries in different careers.

If you're interested in a career that requires postgraduate training in order to qualify with a professional association, look on the organisation's website to find out what will be required after your degree. You could also investigate future job opportunities and likely salaries.

If you're interested in a subject that doesn't lead directly to a specific career (e.g. history or sociology), a good starting point is to find out which careers have been entered by graduates in these subjects. This information is usually available on university and college websites. Find the subject department and look up destinations of recent graduates. It will also be useful to find out how many of last year's graduates are in full-time professional occupations that draw on their particular skills and abilities.

In addition to looking at university and college websites, you could consult the latest edition of *What do graduates do?* which is jointly produced by Jisc and the Association of Graduate Careers Advisory Services (AGCAS). The report, which gives the destinations of students who graduated in 2019 15 months after graduation, is available at https://luminate.prospects.ac.uk/what-do-graduates-do.

Better still, try to find information on graduates' destinations one or two years on, if universities and colleges are able to provide this. Again, university and college websites could be useful here – take a look at the individual subject departments. If they have former students who are in particularly interesting jobs, you can be sure they'll want to show where their courses can lead.

If you have no idea at all

If you're not sure what subject area interests you and you don't have a particular career in mind, it may be worth reconsidering whether higher education is right for you. On the other hand, if you're simply feeling bewildered by the number of options available to you, there are plenty of books (Trotman's *Getting into* series can give some useful insights into career pathways), websites and online tools that can help you to assess your interests. Try a range of them, and take it from there.

TIP!

Remember – your careers adviser is always a good starting point.

The graduate skill set

Some courses lead naturally into a recognised career or occupational area (e.g. engineering, hospitality management, law and medicine), but most don't. So, for many, the benefit of higher education in terms of career prospects is to develop a 'graduate skill set', because study of any subject at this level should develop your abilities in some of the areas employers value, while practical opportunities can help you to develop other valuable skills.

Employers recruit graduates as they value the skills they have developed during their studies, such as:

- planning and organising their work
- time management
- researching facts and broader issues
- understanding and analysing information
- problem solving, critical and logical thinking
- writing well-structured reports, essays, etc.
- giving presentations
- putting forward arguments to support a case in a debate.

These skills are transferable and relevant to a wide range of jobs. Employers also look for other skills and qualities such as motivation and enthusiasm, self-reliance, adaptability, computer literacy, communication (speaking and listening), teamworking and leadership skills. Such skills may be developed during your time at university – either through your course or other activities.

The *Education and Skills Survey*, published by the CBI (Confederation of British Industry) and Pearson Education, reports views from employers on which skills are important to possess for people leaving school, college or university.

'Qualifications are valued by employers as indicators of achievement and ability but developing the right attitudes and behaviours for success in all aspects of life is vital. The evidence

*for this is clear in the survey findings, over half of employers (60%)
value broader skills, such as listening and problem-solving, as one of
their three most important considerations when recruiting school and
college leavers. Furthermore, almost half (45%) of businesses rank
readiness for work as the single most important factor. Even when
considering the value of qualifications, nearly three quarters (74%) of
the businesses say they prefer a mixture of academic and technical
qualifications, or that they view all qualifications equally.'*

*Reproduced with kind permission. Read the survey in full at
www.cbi.org.uk/media/1171/cbi-educating-for-the-modern-world.pdf.*

Attitude and aptitude for work: what are these skills?

They are often known as non-technical, soft, transferable or employability skills. They have different names in different organisations, but
generally come under the following headings:

- business and customer awareness
- communication and literacy
- critical thinking
- entrepreneurship/enterprise
- IT
- managing complex information
- numeracy
- positive attitude
- problem solving
- research skills
- self-management
- team working.

To quote from another important organisation, Stephen Isherwood,
Chief Executive of the Institute of Student Employers, says:

*'Employers want to hire graduates with a mix of knowledge, skills
and abilities plus a meaningful interest in the work that they do.
The language will differ from employer to employer but essentially
employers seek those with:*

- *people skills to get work done with others*
- *practical intelligence to solve problems*
- *resilience to deal with difficult situations*
- *flexibility to deal with change*
- *self-awareness to keep developing as a person*
- *drive and motivation to do the job.*

*'All of these attributes you will hone on the job, but to get the job
you need to show your potential. That can be done through work
experience, internships, volunteering and part-time jobs as long as
you reflect on your experiences and articulate your abilities through
the application process.'*

Many degree and diploma programmes help you to develop these skills. Use the UCAS search tool to check your chosen course at several different universities and colleges, or look at apprenticeship opportunities in UCAS' Career Finder, to learn about the skills they could help you develop. The careers advisory services may also be able to assist. They are there to help students in all years, and making early contact can be very useful.

Many universities and colleges include relevant modules in all their courses and issue students with a logbook or certificate that shows how they gained each skill – for example:

- analysis and solving problems
- team working and interpersonal skills
- verbal communication
- written communication
- personal planning and organising
- initiative
- numerical reasoning
- information literacy and IT.

Plus, many careers services or employability centres run separate employability and personal development courses, which you can follow while working for your academic qualifications. These are well worth exploring when you arrive at university or college – you'll normally receive an award valued by many graduate employers.

Many careers advisory services also run special sessions for students to help them understand which transferable skills are most in demand by employers, and how to acquire them. Some workshops are run by major employers in conjunction with careers advisory services, while others are run independently by careers advisers and focus on subjects such as:

- assessment centres
- commercial awareness
- numbers for the world of work (designed to give confidence in numeracy)
- how to raise your profile when networking online
- industry insights
- successful meetings
- perfect presentations
- realising your strengths
- interview skills
- preparing for psychometric assessment
- project management
- putting your skills to work
- success in business
- team and leadership development.

Having high-level skills in these areas will increase your appeal to prospective employers. With severe competition for the best graduate jobs, employers are able to pick and choose who they hire. So you might like to see what's offered in the way of employability skills training before you make your final choice of course and university or college.

However, some university and college admissions tutors – and some graduate employers – will require you to have demonstrated your interest in your chosen career area through work experience or work placements **before you apply for a higher education place through UCAS**. This is a major reason why it's important to think hard about your career aspirations as early as possible.

Work experience

For many courses, being able to write about suitable work experience on your UCAS form will boost your application. Many courses (especially those linked with health or social care and with careers in the land-based industries, for example) nearly always expect applicants to have arranged some experience – even for a short period – in a relevant job. Maybe your school or college is already on to this and has arranged some form of work experience or shadowing for you? If not, you could try to arrange something yourself to take place in the holidays.

Even one or two days spent in gaining relevant experience or in work shadowing can be helpful.

What is work shadowing?

This term refers to observing someone at work – normally in a highly skilled job. A solicitor, dentist or surgeon for instance might let a student spend some time with them (though wouldn't have the knowledge yet to try out the job!). A good shadowing period would though allow you to learn by watching and asking questions.

Try some or all of the following:

- look for the type of business you'd like to work for (for example, solicitors, hospitals, etc.)
- make a list of the companies you'd like to work for
- make a note of their contact details – you can usually get these details online
- ask if they have any work experience opportunities by email; it's a good idea to phone first and ask who to contact.

If they don't have any opportunities at the time, you could ask if they could contact you when something comes up next – and offer to send them a copy of your CV (a document that lists your personal information, education and experience; this is sometimes also known as a résumé, though this is primarily a North American term).

Writing a CV

A CV should include:

- your full name
- your address
- contact details – phone number and email address
- education – schools/colleges, qualifications, beginning with the most recent
- skills – e.g. knowledge of computer/software packages, driving licence
- previous work experience, giving name of employers
- positions of responsibility in or out of school or college
- interests/hobbies
- names of two or three referees – it is essential you gain permission from the people you list as able to provide a reference.

A CV should be no longer than two sides in length. Use a clear font, like Calibri or Arial, at a minimum font size of 11pt.

Recent research has found that employers spend around 10 seconds reading a CV. So, be concise with language – avoid lengthy sentences or paragraphs and make use of bullet points, e.g. when listing key skills. Plus, always send an accompanying 'cover letter'. See opposite for a sample CV.

Finding work experience

Finding work experience isn't always possible. Some professionals, such as doctors, vets, accountants and lawyers, are often flooded with requests from students. Plus, they have the problem of contacting patients or clients to ask if they'll agree to have a student present. And the Covid-19 pandemic has made finding these sort of work experience opportunities even more difficult.

However, since the Covid-19 pandemic started, there has been a significant growth of virtual internships where people can work with employers from home. Online work experience is open to all, and for the majority of opportunities all you need to get involved is access to a computer and a stable internet connection. Virtual internships are in many ways similar to in-person internships, but their online nature enables participants to work with organisations across the UK and abroad. They are particularly relevant in these unprecedented times, as students and graduates can gain invaluable work experience and boost their CV in spite of coronavirus restrictions. The Prospects UK website is a useful source of information on virtual internships and includes a vacancy search facility.

CHLOE ADAMS
4 The Pines, Anytown, Hampshire, HR51 3DF
07987 123456; ca2005@zmail.com

PERSONAL PROFILE

An A level student of biology, psychology and English literature, looking to make a career as a speech and language therapist. Currently gaining experience supporting primary school pupils with reading skills, including working with a school SEN Co-ordinator. Patient, empathic, approachable, and highly conscientious. Looking for experience in a health setting to enhance my prospects for entry to a degree in speech and language therapy at university.

KEY SKILLS, QUALITIES & EXPERIENCE

- Sensitive to and understanding of others
- Understanding and awareness of how people communicate, including recognising facial expressions and body language; able to adapt to communication needs of children worked with
- Strong attention to detail
- Patient and calm in stressful situations
- Computer literate, proficient in MS Word, ExCel and PowerPoint
- Well-developed written and spoken communication skills

EDUCATION, TRAINING & QUALIFICATIONS

Sept 2021 to date: Anytown Sixth Form College, Hampshire
Studying for GCE A level: Biology, Psychology and English Literature.
GCSEs: English Language (7), English Literature (8), Mathematics (6), Biology (7), Chemistry (6), Physics (6), French (7), Design Technology (6).
A member of the school council in Years 10 and 11. Represented the school at hockey from Years 7 to 11.

WORK EXPERIENCE

October 2021 to date: **Volunteer Support Assistant**, St Peter's Primary School, Anytown, Hampshire
I attend school for half a day per week to assist with reading and writing activities with Year 2 children; this involves one-to-one reading and listening with pupils, assisting with classroom set up and providing general support to teachers as required.
June 2019 to date: **Saturday Cafe Assistant**, The Coffee Shop, Anytown, Hampshire
The role involves taking orders, serving customers, taking payments (cash and card), and preparing refreshments and light meals to order. I gained my Level 2 Food Hygiene Certificate in June 2019.

SOCIAL ACTIVITIES & INTERESTS

Keeping fit and healthy through attendance at local gym, running and swimming.

REFERENCES

Available on request.

If you can't get any experience in the profession you are hoping to enter, there are alternatives. You could, for example, visit law courts and observe different trials. If you can't arrange work experience in a hospital or with a GP, you could try to observe what goes on at a typical doctor's practice. You could ask if it's possible to spend some time with a practice nurse or healthcare assistant.

If you can't find any opportunities in a relevant profession, you could still demonstrate that you have the right sort of personal skills by doing paid or voluntary work in a caring environment where you'll learn to work with people directly, for example:

- in a children's nursery if you're interested in teaching
- in a day centre for people with disabilities if you're interested in nursing, physiotherapy or social work
- with a volunteer agency such as a drug rehabilitation centre or a night shelter for homeless people if you hope to study social work or psychology
- on a local conservation project if you're hoping to do a course connected with the environment.

While you should not do voluntary work just to make your UCAS application look good, it can certainly help to strengthen an application. It can also give you the satisfaction of helping other people and help you to find out a bit more about careers that might interest you. A good place to start is your local volunteer centre, which will have a list of opportunities, or through online databases such as www.doit.life, where you can search for over one million volunteering opportunities by interest, activity or location and apply online.

While in higher education

The same points apply once you get to university or college. You may need to work during term time, so look first for relevant experience. Try to spend time in a job that will broaden your experience and give you insight into a potential employment area. If that's not possible, do your best to draw up a list of transferable skills applicable to any career from any kind of job, e.g. bar work, sales, whatever you can find.

Your university's careers advisory service or student services unit can usually help, and may run a job shop to help students find part-time opportunities. It can also provide details of vacation work placements – and may even be able to give you a grant to help with additional expenses you might incur on a placement.

Describing work experience on your UCAS application

When describing work experience in your personal statement, it is important to explain how the things you did support your application, and also what you learned from the experience gained and, further, what you learned about yourself. This is particularly important for applications for degrees such as medicine or nursing, but can be applied to other areas of study as well. Here is an example:

'One of my work experience placements was in a nursing home – I helped serve teas and befriend elderly residents. The experience really taught me the value of taking time to listen and the importance of treating the elderly with dignity and respect. Many had led fascinating lives which they enjoyed telling me about, and talking about their families. Talking can be a very effective therapy, especially for those who feel isolated from family and get few visitors. This experience helped me build a very positive relationship with the residents and they were always pleased to see me. I have also learned about the need for empathy; trying to put oneself in the position of the other person and seeing things from their viewpoint. I believe that this experience has helped me towards a career in nursing in which compassion, patience and empathy are essential qualities.'

Admissions tutors are interested to see how you dealt with situations encountered during work experience placements with clear examples, not just claiming that you have particular qualities or skills.

Source: Ray Le Tarouilly from UCAS Higher Education Conference
Workshop on Degrees in Health-Based Subjects

TIP!

Admissions tutors are impressed by applicants who have built up knowledge of a related work sector and whose plans include developing useful employment links while studying. If you tried hard to obtain work experience but were unsuccessful, explain this on your UCAS application and describe related activities that you have undertaken as an alternative.

Case study - Deb

At the time of writing, Deb is a second year student reading a sociology and criminology joint degree.

'I chose *what* to study at university based on my interest in sociology at A level. Right now, I don't have any set ideas about what my future career will be, although hopefully it will be connected to the criminal justice system – perhaps criminal rehabilitation or probation work. I loved sociology at A level, and I was hungry to learn more about why people commit crime and the effect it has on society.

'I chose *where* to study based on the enthusiasm of the lecturing staff I met at an open day. I found their talks about the research they were doing so interesting, and when I saw that the course involved visits from people who had experienced the criminal justice system themselves, as well as people who work in the system, I thought this course would be a great opportunity to get a real insight into the causes of criminal behaviour and how people manage to turn their lives around. I was also attracted to the small group sizes of seminar groups, as this allows for discussion of topics with other students and lecturers. We did lots of this on my A level sociology course too and I really enjoyed this way of learning. We were taught to challenge ideas, and I have learned how to analyse and not accept things at face value.

'Everyone is different and we all have our own priorities and preferences, but my advice to people choosing universities and courses is to get a good understanding of the course, how it is taught, how it is assessed and how comfortable you feel with the overall set up of the university. It really is important to visit the place if you possibly can. Virtual events and websites can give a glossy picture of what universities are like; it's only by visiting them that you get a real idea of what they are like, as well as the surrounding area.

'I chose the university that was really helpful and quick to respond to my questions at all stages of my application journey. Other places were less helpful, and didn't feel right for me.

'This degree is equipping me with a lot of useful skills, including data analysis, report writing and effective listening, all of which can be used in all sorts of careers.'

Chapter summary

It's helpful to have a career path in mind, even if it might change later as you progress through your course and gain experience. The earlier you start your research, the better your chance of making an informed decision – with the added benefit that evidence of your long-term approach will strengthen your UCAS application and help you give a good interview.

Resources

Publications

- *Getting into* series, Trotman Education, www.trotman.co.uk. Gives advice on securing a place at university for courses leading to professional careers (such as medicine, law, psychology, physiotherapy, engineering, pharmacy, veterinary school, and business and management courses), and on gaining places on courses at Oxford and Cambridge.
- *HEAP 2023: University Degree Course Offers*, Brian Heap, Trotman Education, www.trotman.co.uk.
- *How to Write a Winning UCAS Personal Statement*, Trotman Education, www.trotman.co.uk.
- *If Only I'd Known: Making the most of higher education, a guide for students and parents*, Association of Graduate Recruiters, www.qualityresearchinternational.com. Contains tips on making the most of higher education and how to gain the skills that will increase your employability.
- *STEM Careers*, Trotman Education, www.trotman.co.uk.
- *What do graduates do?*, Jisc and Association of Graduate Careers Advisory Services (AGCAS), https://luminate.prospects.ac.uk/what-do-graduates-do.
- *You're Hired! CV*, Trotman, www.trotman.co.uk.
- *You're Hired! Graduate Career Handbook*, Trotman, www.trotman.co.uk.

Online tools

- Kudos – information on careers and higher education courses, together with case studies and articles. This may be available in your school or college, at your local careers service or library (CASCAiD, www.cascaid.co.uk).
- The Morrisby Profile – assesses aptitudes, personality and interests to provide a highly reliable predictor of career matches and resources to help research further and higher education options. Online activity only. Details at www.morrisby.com.

- MyUniChoices – a preference-based questionnaire which gives recommended university subjects to explore (www.myunichoices.com).
- UCAS Careers Quiz – find your ideal job matched to your personality and a list of courses previous students studied in order to get there (www.ucas.com/careers-quiz).

The following resources may be available at your school, college, careers centre or library.

- eCLIPS – allows users to search for careers against criteria such as work skills or school subjects, and also has a linked interest guide and information on over 1,200 jobs and careers (www.eclips-online.co.uk).
- Job Explorer Database (Jed) – an interactive, multimedia careers information resource where you can explore over 800 jobs in depth (2,500 individual career titles), with pictures and case studies of people at work. The section 'Higher ideas' shows which higher education courses connect with interests and subject choices (Careersoft, www.careersoft.co.uk).

Websites

- https://indigo.careers – extensive subscription-based careers advice site that may be available at your school, college, careers centre or library.
- www.agcas.org.uk – Association of Graduate Careers Advisory Services.
- www.doit.life – a national database of volunteering opportunities where you can search by postcode and interests for opportunities in your local area.
- https://nationalcareersservice.direct.gov.uk – search under 'job profiles'; the site contains over 800 listings. The site also offers guidance on the employability of various degree subjects and suggests different skills that specific degrees can add to your CV.
- www.prospects.ac.uk – useful detailed information on graduate careers.
- www.thestudentroom.co.uk – a site where students can share experiences on all sorts of education-based topics, including tips on writing the personal statement. However, do not rely solely on this.

3 | A matter of money

If you've come this far in the book, you're serious about applying to a higher education institution. Though, even before considering whether you're likely to achieve the entry grades for the course, you'll probably have asked yourself, 'Can I afford it?'

Certainly, you'll need to think through your finances very carefully and research all the types of assistance that's available to you. There is a lot of information available on government websites, on ucas.com, from universities and colleges and in books written specifically on this subject. A summary is given in this chapter, with details of where to look for more information in the 'Resources' section at the end.

To help you consider whether higher education is right for you, this chapter looks at the two main costs in attending higher education: tuition fees and living expenses.

All figures given in this chapter were current in May 2022. You can expect increases in future years – you'll need to check for up-to-date rates.

Tuition fees

The cost of providing college and university courses is met partly by the government and partly through variable tuition fees, which are the student's contribution.

Those who are resident or have had settled status in the UK for at least 3 years can apply for a government tuition fee loan. For UK students, the fees don't have to be paid at the start of each year. You're effectively given a loan by the government that you repay through your income tax when your earnings reach a certain level – for 2023 entry students this is £25,000 per annum for students in England, Wales and Scotland, and £19,895 for students in Northern Ireland. However, if you never reach these thresholds, you will not have to repay the fees. The reader is advised to check with the student finance site for the region of the UK in which they live for updates on student finance for higher education.

The tuition fees you'll have to pay for undergraduate courses will depend on where you live and where you intend to study. However, £9,250 is the maximum that universities are currently permitted to charge for higher education courses, aside from accelerated degree courses (usually two years as opposed to three years), in which case they are permitted to charge up to £11,100 per year.

England

Students living in England have to pay a maximum of £9,250 per year if they are studying in England, Scotland or Northern Ireland, or up to £9,000 if they study in Wales.

Scotland

Students from Scotland who study at Scottish universities don't pay tuition fees. They'll have to pay fees of up to £9,250 if they study in England or Northern Ireland, or up to £9,000 if they study in Wales.

Northern Ireland

Students living in Northern Ireland have to pay up to £4,530 if they attend a university in Northern Ireland, or up to £9,250 if they study in England or Scotland, or up to £9,000 if they study in Wales.

Wales

Students from Wales pay up to £9,000 if they study in Wales, or £9,250 if they study in England, Scotland or Northern Ireland.

EU and international students

EU and international students pay higher fees, determined by each university. According to the *Times Higher Education* (THE) magazine, undergraduate tuition fees for an international student in 2020 were between £10,000 and £26,000 per year. A longer undergraduate degree such as medicine can cost foreign students almost £59,000. Generally speaking, humanities and social science courses cost the least, while laboratory and clinical degrees are more expensive.

EU and international students are not eligible for UK student loans. Prospective students are advised to regularly check the student finance sites for all four of the constituent UK countries for up-to-date information and sites of higher education institutions that they are considering applying to for details of tuition fees.

Full details and information on loans and grants can be found at www.gov.uk/browse/education/student-finance.

TIP!

You're advised to apply to the appropriate authority for funding as soon as you have firmly accepted an offer of a place.

Living expenses

Your living expenses include the cost of your accommodation, food, clothes, travel, books and equipment, leisure and social activities – plus possible extras like field trips and study visits, if these aren't covered by the tuition fees.

It's impossible to suggest a standard amount for living expenses since they vary at different universities, colleges and locations. Also, individual students' tastes, needs and priorities vary widely. Costs also vary for different types of accommodation – this is the factor that will most affect your expenditure. Some accommodation is luxury standard with on-site launderette, cinema, gym, games rooms and bars, etc., which will be very expensive. Not every option below is available at every university or college, but you might be able to choose between:

- a study bedroom in a hall of residence with an en suite bathroom
- a standard room, usually fitted with a hand basin, and shared baths/ showers and lavatories
- a shared room (not as widely available) – there can be as much as £3,000 per year difference between the cost of an en suite bedroom and a shared room
- meals provided – in halls, usually dinner and breakfast but some also provide lunch
- self-catering accommodation – i.e. with a shared kitchen with fridge, cooker, cupboards, etc. where you can prepare your own meals
- a room rented from a private landlord, often in a house or apartment shared with other students.

Many first-year students opt for the greater degree of privacy given by an en suite bathroom, but from their second year onwards choose to share private houses with friends they made during their first year. Bathrooms are then shared as are kitchens and cooking facilities. Most first-year students live in a hall of residence which is university managed. Aside from being generally cheaper than private rented accommodation, halls also give the opportunity to make new friends more easily and there is generally better access to student support services. Often there will be a resident warden and/or more senior students who keep a look out for first-years. Starting university in private rented accommodation can lead to early isolation and other problems, so think carefully about how you might cope if you do decide to live outside of university accommodation.

The information below gives you some idea of possible expenses.

- Check university and college websites. Some are better than others and give breakdowns under various headings such as accommodation, food and daily travel. Others go further and give typical weekly, monthly or annual spends. They don't give this information in a standard format, though – the figures could be weekly, monthly or for an academic or calendar year. You'll want to compare like with like. Are you interested in figures for term time only or term time plus Easter and Christmas holidays (particularly if you are an international student and not likely to go home then)? Or for a whole year if you think you might stay in your university or college town for 12 months?

- When considering accommodation it is also important to check things like:
  - o is personal property insurance included in accommodation fees?
  - o is there free wifi in the bedrooms?
  - o will a television licence also be included or will you have to pay for your own?
  - o if you don't want to pay for an entire year's accommodation will you have to pay a small fee to keep your room reserved for you during Christmas and Easter vacations?
  - o if you choose self-catering accommodation how many students share a kitchen?

- You'll probably be surprised when you do some research to find that the cheapest and most expensive towns are not as you might have expected. Much depends on how much accommodation is available and how much daily travel costs come to.

- According to the National Union of Students and Unipol, the average cost for weekly rent in the UK in purpose-built student accommodation in 2021/22 was £166. Private sector accommodation averaged £8,002 per year, compared to university-owned and -managed accommodation which averaged £6,227 a year. In London, the average rent was £8,984 per year for university accommodation and £12,382 for the private sector. Small variations in weekly rent add up to a significant amount over the course of a year. Many students opt to study where it's cheaper, e.g. Wales, and save over £2,000 a year compared with London. However, if you intend to take a term-time job, note that average wages in London will often be higher than in other parts of the country.

- The NUS (www.nus.org.uk) gives average costs for a 39-week academic year in towns throughout England. There is also useful information on costs of student living on the *Which?* website: www.which.co.uk/money/university-and-student-finance/student-money-and-budgeting/how-much-it-costs-to-live-at-university.

TIP!

Many universities have accommodation brochures online. In some towns a large amount of student accommodation is owned by private companies as opposed to the universities and colleges themselves. This option means you could potentially be sharing accommodation with students from other universities and colleges.

Funding your studies

How do you intend to fund your time in higher education? Don't ignore this question and leave it until the last minute! You'll need to think carefully about how to budget for several years' costs – and you need to know what help you might get from:

- the Government
- your family or partner
- other sources.

The National Money Survey 2021, conducted by Save the Student, found that 66% of students rely on part time employment to supplement their income, a drop from 74% in the previous year. This is in part due to a reduction in job vacancies owing to the Covid pandemic. Further, 66% rely on help from their parents, a slight decrease from the previous year's figure of 68%. In addition, 38% rely on non-repayable grants and bursaries, a drop from 44% in 2020.

Interestingly, since 2020, the proportion of students that make money from cryptocurrencies, such as Bitcoin and Ethereum, has tripled – from 2% to 6%. However, there has been some concern in the media that young people are investing in crypto without a full understanding of the risks involved in these trades.

This chapter gives a brief overview of a complicated funding situation, which can vary according to where you come from and where you plan to study. For more details about all the different types of funding available and how to apply for them, please check your regional student finance website:

- www.gov.uk/contact-student-finance-england
- www.saas.gov.uk
- www.studentfinanceni.co.uk
- www.studentfinancewales.co.uk.

Tuition fee loans

These are available in England, Northern Ireland and Wales. If you take one out (and most students do), the Student Loans Company will pay your fees directly to your university or college at the start of each year of your course, adding the interest to your repayable loan total. The loan will be repaid through the income tax system. This means that once you are working, your employer will take the required amount from your salary and make the payments. The current situation regarding repayments means that you'll:

- repay 9% of anything you earn annually above £25,000 in England, Scotland and Wales, and above £19,895 in Northern Ireland
- repay more than 9% on a sliding scale when you earn over £45,000

- reduce or stop your repayments if you take a pay cut or lose your job
- have your debt cancelled if you have not cleared it by 40 years after graduation.

The interest rate is reviewed each September, and is normally based on the previous March's RPI (Retail Prices Index) rate of inflation plus 3%. In January 2022 the RPI was 7.8%. Though, by the time you read this, this figure might have changed if the bank base rate has increased or decreased. (The Retail Prices Index is a measure of UK inflation; it measures changes to the cost of living in the UK.)

You are advised to keep a close watch on developments in student finance. In early 2022 the government introduced changes that included extending the repayment period limit from 30 to 40 years for all students starting university from 2023 onwards.

Maintenance or living costs loans

In addition to a tuition fee loan, all students can apply for a maintenance or living cost loan. The maximum amount available per year is £12,382, which is based on what a student from England might receive if studying in London. Figures for students from Wales, Scotland and Northern Ireland will vary slightly. All students are entitled to a maintenance loan; however, part of this amount will be dependent on your household income – in other words, it is means-tested. 'Household income' refers to your family's gross annual income (their income before tax) of the household you live in. Certain pension contributions and allowances for dependent children are also deducted from the figure to achieve the total sum.

Each regional student finance site includes a finance calculator tool that will give an estimate of the finance you would be eligible for based on family income and other factors, and it is well worth you using this before starting university.

England (2022-23)

The maximum annual loan in England:

- £8,171 for those living in the family home
- £9,706 for those studying away from home (£12,667 in London)
- £11,116 for students spending at least one term of a UK course overseas.

Northern Ireland (2022-23)

The maximum annual loan in Northern Ireland:

- £3,750 for those living in the family home
- £4,840 for those studying away from home (£6,780 in London)
- £5,770 for students spending a year of a UK course overseas.

A lower maintenance loan is paid in the final year of study. In addition, a non repayable maintenance grant is available if your household income is below £41,065 and it is paid to you. This is paid alongside any maintenance loan you qualify for and is up to £3,475.

Wales (2022-23)

In Wales students can get a combination of a maintenance grant and a maintenance loan. Although the grants are means tested, most students will get a Welsh Government Learning Grant of at least £1,000 per year.

Maximum sums for maintenance loans and grants in Wales:

- £6,885 grant for those living in the family home
- £8,100 grant for those studying away from home (£10,124 in London)
- For students spending a year of a UK course overseas, please refer to Student Finance Wales (www.studentfinancewales.co.uk) for details of grants for studying abroad.

Scotland (2022-23)

In Scotland students can get a mix of maintenance loans and means-tested bursaries (grants) to cover living costs. These are as follows (all figures per year):

- household income up to £20,999: £2,000 bursary and £6,100 loan
- household income £21,000–£23,999: £1,125 bursary and £6,100 loan
- household income £24,000–£33,999: £500 bursary and £6,100 loan
- household income £34,000 and above: no bursary and £5,100 loan.

Maintenance loans are repaid in the same way as loans for tuition fees. Extra help may be available for students with disabilities and for those on low incomes or who have dependants.

Applying

According to Student Finance England, students can follow a few simple steps to try and ensure their application is processed as quickly as possible, including:

- make a note of your account log-in details and keep them safe
- make sure any evidence and information needed to support your application is supplied 'right first time' (students and family/partners)
- submit an application even if there's a delay in getting sponsor income details so some funding will be available when you start your course
- read, understand and agree to the terms and conditions of your student loan before submitting an application.

Additional support

Bursaries and scholarships

What's the difference? Bursaries are usually non-competitive and auto-matic, often based on financial need, while scholarships are competitive and you usually have to apply for them. However, many universities and colleges use the terms interchangeably.

As well as the funding described above, most universities and colleges offer tuition fee bursaries, mainly to students who receive the maximum maintenance loan. These bursaries cover part or all of the cost of the course and are awarded according to the universities' own criteria, but they are often worked out according to the level of parental income. Approximately one-third of students receive some kind of financial assistance in this way.

Some universities and colleges offer scholarships to students enrolling on certain courses **or** to students with the highest entry grades. Merit-based scholarships and prizes are also sometimes available once you have started university, for example, if you have performed particularly well in end-of-year examinations.

Students leaving care

Care leavers are eligible to apply for a bursary of at least £2,000 from their local authority area; this may be paid to them as a lump sum or in instalments. Many universities and colleges offer further support and are often able to provide accommodation for the whole year – which means that students don't have to move out during vacations. Find out more at ucas.com/care-leavers.

Other help from universities and colleges

Not all help comes in the form of cash. Students may receive any of the following – again probably dependent on income:

- assistance with cost of compulsory field trips and visits
- help to purchase laboratory clothing
- free laptops.

Additional financial support may be available to students with disabili-ties, for those with dependants and for mature students with existing financial commitments. These regulations are subject to change so it is essential to check them.

Other bursaries and scholarships

Students on particular courses, with particular career aspirations or with particular personal circumstances may be eligible for extra financial help. It's worth checking the sources listed at the end of this chapter to find out whether you might be eligible for a grant made by a particular professional organisation or charity.

Sponsorship

Students applying for particular courses – for example accountancy, business studies and engineering – can sometimes be sponsored by employers or related organisations. In return for a sum of money paid to you as a student you would normally be expected to work for your sponsor during some of your vacations. Naturally, if you were suitable they would expect you to work for them for a period after you graduated. (However, the number of sponsorships available to new students has declined. Many employers now prefer to sponsor students whom they select during the first or second year of their courses.)

Degree and Higher apprenticeships

Degree apprenticeships involve studying for a degree or postgraduate level qualification. Higher apprenticeships involve studying for a qualification such as a Foundation degree, Higher National Diploma or other professional qualification equivalent to these, although in some cases Higher apprenticeships can lead to the award of a degree.

Degree apprentices don't pay for training or tuition fees – these are covered by the employer and the government. You will be paid a wage throughout the course, which will help to cover your living costs. Degree apprentices aren't entitled to student loans.

NHS bursaries

Students on degree courses in medicine and dentistry are treated in the same way as students on other degree programmes for the first four years of their courses. Then, from the fifth year, there's NHS funding to assist with tuition and living expenses. These bursaries are income-related. The system is not the same for all parts of the UK, so check your national student finance websites.

TIP!

Make a note of any deadlines for loan or funding applications and ensure that you have completed all the forms in time.

Other sources of cash

Part-time work

Many students need to balance studies with part-time employment. One report showed that the annual average amount earned was £3,500. This is something to think about when you choose your universities and colleges. Some towns have many more opportunities than others. In an area of high unemployment, for instance, all the jobs may be taken by permanent workers. In more affluent areas there might be more hourly paid work available – especially at hours when students are willing to work. At the time of writing, employers in sectors such as retail, hospitality, warehousing and care are struggling to recruit staff in many areas of the country; depending on location, jobs are relatively plentiful. There are also more opportunities to work from home, so IT skills are useful to keep up to date. You can find free digital courses by using the National Careers Service website; see link: https://nationalcareers.service.gov.uk/find-a-course/the-skills-toolkit.

You can check out the local employment situation on university and college websites.

Here are some additional ideas to bear in mind.

- Many universities and colleges help by running their own jobs banks. Students can get work, for example, in the Students' Union, libraries or offices (secretarial and administrative work if they have the skills), or in catering, domestic or manual work.
- Other opportunities often include guiding visitors around the campus or acting as student guides on open days.
- Most universities and colleges also have a job shop provided by student services or the careers advisory service that advertises jobs in the town or city.
- A useful website with a number of part-time jobs is www.fish4.co.uk.

However, many higher education courses include practical coursework, field studies and/or time spent abroad, which leave little opportunity for employment during term time. Plus, it's often recommended that students spend no more than 15 hours a week in paid employment to make sure their studies don't suffer. Oxford and Cambridge don't encourage any of their students to work during term time.

If you are an international student, you'll need to check the wording on your visa regarding part-time work. It may say that you are not permitted to undertake paid work at all, or perhaps only for a certain number of hours each week or month.

TIP!

Check the cost of living and employment availability in the university towns you're interested in. This will help you estimate what your living costs are likely to be and the availability of part-time work.

Banking deals

Many students take advantage of the student banking deals available from a number of high street banks. These can include interest-free overdrafts (which are advisable as a last resort only because they do have to be repaid – and interest rates on late payments can be very high) as well as various other freebies like free driving lessons or rail-cards. Shop around carefully for the deal that best suits your priorities – and remember, the advice that banks give on their websites is unlikely to be wholly impartial.

Many universities and colleges have student financial advisers whom students can approach for help. A students' union is also a good source of information and advice on financial assistance.

TIP!

Try not to run up a large overdraft or credit card debts, as in the long run you can end up paying large sums of interest on the money owed.

Chapter summary

Money can be a major headache for students, so it is well worth taking the time to work out how you're going to fund yourself. It's also very important to be on top of all the paperwork required for loan applications because missed deadlines can mean that you start your course before your finance comes through.

Resources

Publications

- Various Child Poverty Action Group titles, for example *Welfare Benefits and Tax Credits Handbook*, *Student Support and Benefits Handbook*, *Council Tax Handbook* and *Child Support Handbook*, for England, Wales and Northern Ireland; most are available online at www.cpag.org.uk.

- For Scottish residents, as above plus *Benefits for Students in Scotland Handbook*, available from Child Poverty Action Group in Scotland at www.cpag.org.uk/scotland.

Official organisations

- www.gov.uk/contact-student-finance-england.
- www.gov.uk/education/student-grants-bursaries-scholarships.
- www.gov.uk/extra-money-pay-university – for information on bursaries and scholarships.
- www.gov.uk/student-finance-calculator – helps you to estimate which loans and other sources of funding you might be able to get.
- www.saas.gov.uk.
- www.studentfinanceni.co.uk.
- www.studentfinancewales.co.uk.

General student support

- www.becomecharity.org.uk – for young care leavers.
- www.moneysavingexpert.com/students – the site of money expert Martin Lewis, which gives helpful advice on student budgeting.
- https://nationalcareers.service.gov.uk/find-a-course/the-skills-toolkit.
- www.nhsbsa.nhs.uk/nhs-bursary-students – information on NHS student bursaries.
- www.nus.org.uk – the National Union of Students.
- www.propel.org.uk – a specialist website for prospective students leaving care.
- www.slc.co.uk – the Student Loans Company.
- www.studying-in-uk.org.
- www.studyinternational.com.
- www.thescholarshiphub.org.uk – information on possible bursaries, scholarships, sponsors and degree apprenticeships.
- www.ucas.com/money – you can also contact UCAS through Facebook and Twitter.
- www.which.co.uk/money/university-and-student-finance/student-money-and-budgeting/how-much-it-costs-to-live-at-university.

Part-time and temporary jobs

- www.e4s.co.uk.
- www.fish4.co.uk.
- www.student-jobs.co.uk.
- www.timewisejobs.co.uk
- www.uktemps.co.uk

4 | Choosing what to study

You're probably already aware that there's a vast number of subjects on offer. You can get an idea of the full range by searching ucas.com and the other resources listed on page 45.

You can enter up to five course choices on your UCAS application. However, if you are applying for medicine, dentistry or veterinary science you're limited to four courses in your chosen subject, although you can make one additional application to a course in another subject (see Chapter 8 for more information).

So how do you start to narrow it down? This chapter covers some of the questions you can ask yourself so that you can focus your research on the courses that suit your interests.

Which subject area?

You might already have an idea of what you'd like to pursue further. If not, here are a few questions to think about.

- Which of the subjects you are currently studying interests you most? Are you interested enough to want to study it for the next few years?
- Are you interested in one particular aspect of your advanced-level course? If so, some specialist higher education courses could allow you to focus on this particular aspect.
- What are your career plans? What are the entry requirements for that career? Which courses match this best?
- Are you prepared to potentially undertake more specific job-related training once you have graduated? If not, perhaps you should be looking for a vocational (career-related) course that leads directly into an occupation.

The following online tools can help you choose a course. They might be available for you to use at your school, college or local careers centre.

Higher Ideas

Find out which higher education courses tie in with your interests and school subject choices, and from there read about:

- course content
- which universities and colleges offer them
- what qualifications you might need
- how to find out more.

Search over 41,000 courses across the different UK regions. This site also has a link to the Job Explorer Database referred to in Chapter 2.

The Morrisby Profile

This is an online activity comprising a range of psychometric aptitude tests and preference-based questions. These give an indication of your learning potential and the most effective ways that you are likely to use your skills. Some schools and colleges use the profile as a guidance tool for students age 15+.

As well as career recommendations, Morrisby also identifies A level and university course suggestions and has online careers materials you can use in your research. There are advisers who will provide a post-assessment guidance service to individual clients as well as institutions, on a fee-paying basis. See www.morrisby.com/morrisby-profile for further details.

MyUniChoices

Find courses that might appeal to you by completing an online question-naire – which is used to assess your interests, abilities and personal qualities. This assessment matches your replies with thousands of higher education courses in the UK, Ireland, Europe and Canada – at mainly degree, HND or Diploma levels.

MyUniChoices asks you:

- 150 questions about what you do and do not like
- what stage you are at with your current academic studies
- which courses and subjects you are taking now or planning to take.

You'll receive a list of courses to investigate and an action plan suggest-ing further research. It may challenge your existing ideas and point you towards courses you have not considered. If it's not available to use at school or college, the cost to access this site yourself is £29.99.

The 'Resources' section at the end of Chapter 2 should give you some more ideas of where to start your research.

The UCAS Hub and Careers Quiz

Register for the UCAS Hub on ucas.com – your starting point to explore, research and chat to current students. After registration there is no obligation to apply and you can explore a wide range of options. The

UCAS Careers Quiz will help you find your ideal job matched to your personality, and give you a list of courses previous students studied in order to get there at www.ucas.com/careers-quiz.

Which qualification?

It is important to know something about each of the different types of qualification on offer so that you can choose one that's right for you. For example, course lengths (and therefore expenses) vary widely. Here are some of the main options.

DipHEs

Some universities and colleges offer undergraduate courses leading to a DipHE (Diploma of Higher Education). Two-year full-time DipHE courses are normally equivalent to the first two years of a first or bachelor's degree, and can often be used for entry to the final year of a related degree course. They're mainly linked to performance or vocational areas such as animal studies, dance education, health and social care, and paramedic practice – although some universities and colleges offer them in humanities subjects, including English and history.

HNDs

A Higher National Diploma (HND) is a vocational qualification roughly equivalent to the first two years of a three-year degree course.

Many universities and colleges offer HND courses in the same subject areas as their degree courses, giving you the option to transfer between courses or to top up your HND to a degree through a further year's study. In fact the majority of students do this, either by taking a special one-year top-up course or by transferring to the second or third year of a degree course in a similar subject at their university or college. Keep this in mind when planning your application strategy.

HNDs often fall into two main subject areas: science, construction, engineering and technology, and business studies and related subjects. Although HNDs do exist in art and design, health and social care, performing arts and hospitality management.

Science, construction, engineering and technology

Courses at all levels in these categories attract comparatively fewer applications than business and finance courses. It's therefore likely that if you apply for a degree in, for example, mechanical engineering at an institution that also offers an HND in engineering, admissions tutors will make you an offer covering both the degree and the HND course, but with different entry conditions for each (normally lower for the HND).

Business studies and related subjects

The HND courses in this subject area usually attract a large number of applications in their own right: many students choose HND courses because they are shorter and often more specialised than the degrees. It's therefore less usual for universities and colleges to make dual offers for degrees and HNDs.

If you have doubts about your ability to reach the level required for degree entry, you could instead apply for the HND. Talk through the options with your teachers or careers adviser.

Foundation degrees

As with HNDs, these courses focus on a particular job or profession. They're available in England, Northern Ireland and Wales. Full-time courses last two years and, like HNDs (which in some subject areas Foundation degrees have replaced), can be converted into honours degrees with a subsequent year of full-time study. Designed by business and industry to meet their skills needs, Foundation degrees were originally developed to train employees in particular roles as higher technicians or associate professionals, but entry to full-time courses is now available to anyone.

Foundation degrees combine academic study with the development of work-related skills. Programmes are offered in areas such as digital media arts, business and management, horticulture, equine studies, hospitality, fashion design and a vast range of other subjects. Foundation degree courses lead to the awards of:

- FdA (arts)
- FdEng (engineering)
- FdSci (science).

Entrance requirements for Foundation degrees vary, but typically are very similar to those required for HNDs: a **minimum** of a pass grade in one A level or equivalent qualification and another subject studied to A level standard but not necessarily passed. However, in some cases entrance requirements can be higher, so please check individual institution entrance requirements carefully.

Degree courses

Bachelor's degrees

In England, Northern Ireland and Wales, first degree courses usually last three years, or four if a year abroad or work placement is included. They lead to the award of a bachelor's degree, with the title of the degree reflecting the subject studied. Some of the more common ones are:

- BA: Bachelor of Arts
- BCom: Bachelor of Commerce
- BEng: Bachelor of Engineering
- BMus: Bachelor of Music
- BSc: Bachelor of Science
- LLB: Bachelor of Law.

The exceptions to this are the universities of Oxford and Cambridge (Oxbridge), which award a BA regardless of the subject. (Oxbridge graduates are then able to upgrade to a master's degree, without further exams, about four years later.)

Entrance requirements for entry to degree courses vary considerably, ranging from two low grade to three top grade A levels or equivalent.

Master's degrees

In England, Northern Ireland and Wales, master's degrees are usually acquired via a completely different course that must be applied for separately and can't be taken until the bachelor's degree has been completed.

However, some first degree courses lead directly to the award of a master's degree (e.g. MEd, MEng, MPhys and MSc). These courses are usually extended or enhanced versions of the bachelor's course, lasting at least four years, and are likely to be in engineering or science disciplines.

Scottish universities and colleges

At Scottish universities and colleges standard bachelor's degrees normally last for four years rather than three, and students typically take a broad range of subjects in the first two years before going on to specialise in the final two years.

At some universities and colleges, students are awarded a master's as standard for a four-year degree in arts, humanities and social science subjects, while science students receive a BSc.

Single, joint or combined honours?

Most universities and colleges offer single, joint and combined honours degree courses. Combined honours courses enable you to combine several areas of interest and may lead you to an interesting programme or additional career opportunities (for example, studying biology with French may enable you to work in France).

It's important to check the weighting given to each subject in a combined course. Popular ones include 50/50 and 75/25. As a general rule you can assume that **Subject A AND Subject B** means equal time given to each whereas **Subject A WITH Subject B** means much less time spent on the second or minor subject. There are some exceptions though, and universities and colleges are able to decide on their own course titles. The best way to be sure you know what you'll be studying is to check course information very carefully.

If you intend to take a joint or combined honours course, you'll be kept busier than you would be on a single honours course. You may have to make your own connections between the modules of study, and the work may not be closely coordinated. Ask the admissions tutors for the subjects you're interested in about the possibilities and potential problems of combining courses.

Degree classification

Honours degrees are classified as:

- First Class
- Upper Second Class (2.i)
- Lower Second Class (2.ii)
- Third Class.

Otherwise, ordinary and pass degrees can be awarded – depending on the system – to students who aren't studying honours courses, or to students who narrowly fail an honours course.

Which mode of study?

While full-time study is the most popular choice, there are also the following options.

Part-time

Part-time study is becoming more popular as students increasingly find it necessary to work in order to finance their studies; on the other hand, it can be difficult to balance the demands of a job and higher education. Make sure you research the practicality of your options before making your decision.

Distance learning

This option was once available only through the Open University, but is now offered by many universities and colleges. This mode of study is more realistic if your circumstances make full-time course attendance difficult, e.g. because of employment or childcare commitments.

A government tuition fee loan is available to study with the Open University and other providers of distance learning, higher education-level qualifications. Repayment is on the same basis as applies to full-time university students.

Sandwich courses

Many degrees and HNDs offer periods of work experience from three to 12 months. The 12-month programmes add a year to your course duration.

Study abroad

Prior to Britain's departure from the European Union on 31 January 2020, many universities in the UK had formal agreements with partner institutions in Europe through the Erasmus+ programme, which enabled UK undergraduate students to apply for courses or work placements in one of 32 other European countries for periods of three to twelve months as part of their degree course. Following Britain's departure from the European Union on 31 January 2020, the UK government replaced the Erasmus+ programme with the Turing Scheme from September 2021. The Turing Scheme is a study and work abroad programme, and will apply to countries across the world. It aims to send approximately 35,000 students on study and work placements overseas each year, and hopes to particularly help disadvantaged students to take advantage of the scheme. Students taking part may receive grants to support their international experience. For further information, see www.turing-scheme.org.uk.

Sponsored study

Sponsorship is sometimes offered to students on certain courses. In some cases students apply for a degree or HND course through UCAS and the university or college helps to arrange their training placement. (Full sponsorship is becoming rarer however, since, increasingly, employers are offering sponsorship only from the second year of a course. It's important, therefore, to check which ones have links with particular universities and colleges.)

If a sponsor requires you to attend a particular university or college, the sponsor will inform you and the institution will sort out the UCAS arrangements.

Degree apprenticeships

Degree apprenticeships are organised differently from sponsorship programmes. They offer the opportunity to gain a full bachelor's degree (and in some cases postgraduate qualifications) through an arrangement between employers and higher education institutions. Part-time study takes place at a university or college, with the rest of your time learning on the job. They can take from three to six years to complete, depending on the course level, and are available in a wide range of sectors. Currently, the scheme is only available in England and Wales, although applications may be made from all parts of the UK.

Use UCAS' Career Finder tool at www.ucas.com/careerfinder to:

- search for all apprenticeship roles
- filter by subject area, role type, location and level of apprenticeship
- sign up for alerts so you don't miss new vacancies.

You can also take a look for vacancies at www.gov.uk/government/publications/higher-and-degree-apprenticeships or on job search websites like www.indeed.co.uk. Availability of degree apprenticeships varies according to locality. The Covid pandemic impacted on vacancy availability, along with jobs and apprenticeships generally, but the gradual removal of lockdown restrictions through 2021 and 2022 led to a resurgence of vacancies.

Entry requirements vary, but in some cases can be very high for getting degree apprenticeships with better known prestigious employers. The big attraction of degree apprenticeships is the prospect of getting a university qualification without any debt. However, universities themselves have said that it is hard work being employed and studying at the same time. You're very likely going to need to give up evenings and some weekends to keep up with study and assignment writing, so this should never be thought of as a soft or easy option.

If you're not sure what you want to do yet, there's nothing stopping you applying to university through UCAS, while also applying for apprenticeship vacancies.

Which courses?

This is, of course, the million-dollar question! Having thought about the above points, you should now have a clearer idea of the type of qualification and subject area you'd like to apply for. However, there may still be hundreds of courses available fitting your criteria – so this is the point where you can start to narrow down your options. The only way to do this is by further research. Take a look through directories, prospectuses and websites, as well as visiting specific departments at specific universities.

Here are some of the things you should take into account.

- **Course content**: there can be a whole world of difference between courses with exactly the same title, so take a detailed look at the content and see how it relates to your particular interests. How much do you want to specialise? How much freedom do you want in selecting your options?
- **Teaching and assessment methods**: again, these can vary widely. For example, some courses may be very practical, with workshops and case studies, while others may be centred on essays and tutorials. If you don't perform well in exams, you can search for courses assessed via modules and projects.

- **Professional accreditation**: if you're planning to enter a specific career which you need professional accreditation for (e.g. law, engineering or accountancy), it is well worth checking out which courses offer full or partial exemption from the exams required to gain this accreditation.
- **Links with industry**: some courses and departments have strong links with industry, which can help graduates secure jobs.
- **Graduate destinations**: these are often listed on university and college websites and can help you assess whether the course will give you the skills you'll need in the workplace.

> **TIP!**
>
> The UCAS search tool enables you to search courses by a wide range of features – including subject, region and town. You can also filter searches by qualification level, study mode, and single or combined subjects. You'll find entry requirements and tuition fees for each courses and links to university and college websites.

Chapter summary

You should now be able to begin to develop a clear idea of the kind of course you'd like to apply for. However, there are two aspects of the decision-making process yet to be discussed: your choice of university or college and entry requirements. These factors are examined in detail in the following chapters.

Resources

Publications

- *Heap 2023: University Degree Course Offers*, Trotman Education, www.trotman.co.uk.
- *The University Choice Journal*, Trotman, www.trotman.co.uk.
- *What do graduates do?*, Jisc and AGCAS, https://luminate. prospects.ac.uk/what-do-graduates-do.

Online tools

- MyUniChoices: www.myunichoices.com.
- Higher Ideas: www.careersoft.co.uk/Products/Higher_Ideas.

Websites

- www.gov.uk/government/publications/higher-and-degree-apprenticeships.
- www.indeed.co.uk.
- https://indigo.careers.
- www.push.co.uk.
- www.telegraph.co.uk/education/universities-colleges.
- www.theguardian.com/education/universityguide.
- www.timeshighereducation.com.
- www.turing-scheme.org.uk.
- www.ucas.com – explore the different course options.

UCAS Discovery events

UCAS organises a wide range of events to give you the chance to explore all your options.

UCAS Discovery online – Start exploring your options online and discover different paths and careers. You can watch and chat live, or catch up on-demand.

UCAS Discovery UK tour – Join UCAS in person to narrow down your choices. Meet representatives from hundreds of universities and employers, and chat face-to-face with students and apprentices.

UCAS Discovery presents – Before making those all-important decisions, take a closer look at the subject or path you're passionate about. Dive into the detail, hear from subject-matter experts, and choose with confidence.

Find out more at ucas.com/ucas/events-exhibitions.

For students interested in pursuing a creative career, UCAS' flagship 'Create your future' events are a unique opportunity to explore hundreds of creative courses, traineeships and careers in design, music and the performing arts.

Taster courses

Many universities and colleges hold taster courses during the summer holidays. If you can manage to attend one you'll get an insight into what life as a student will be like. Courses last from one day to one week and typically include the opportunity to attend lectures and classes, as well as exploring accommodation and the campus. You can search for taster courses at ucas.com/taster-course.

5 | Choosing where to study

The previous chapter hopefully helped you build a picture of your ideal course and start to create a shortlist. However, it's still likely that a lot more than five courses will fit the bill, so you'll need to narrow the list down further. Now's the time to start thinking about which university or college you would like to study at.

Working out your priorities

There are almost 340 institutions in the UCAS application scheme that offer higher education courses – including universities, colleges of higher education and further education colleges. Different consider-ations and priorities affect each person's choice of institution. To give you some idea of the range, current students say they were influenced by one or more of the following factors.

Academic factors

- The type of course you are looking for.
- The reputation for research in a particular department.
- Quality of teaching – check the Teaching Excellence and Student Outcomes Framework document at www.officeforstudents.org.uk/for-students/the-tef.
- The status of the university/college as a whole – you can check league tables, which vary in reliability; however, the *Guardian*, *The Times* and *The Complete University Guide* are more impartial sources (or you could also seek advice from professional bodies and/or employers).
- Entry requirements – be positive but realistic about your potential results at advanced level, so you won't need to revise your plans months later.
- Number of student places on particular courses – the bigger the intake target, usually the better your chances; prospectuses and websites may give an indication of the size of intake.
- Employability of graduates.

Social factors

- Location – do you like the big city or countryside? Do you want to be on a campus or in the middle of a city? Are you trying to stay within easy reach of home, or get as far away as possible?
- Popularity of the university/college.
- Facilities for sport, leisure activities, music, etc.
- Cost of living.
- Accommodation – is there enough available? Does it suit your preferences, e.g. self-catering or with meals provided?
- Financial support available (e.g. bursaries and scholarships).
- Level of support and facilities for students with disabilities.

You may think of more factors, though you'll have to work out which are most important to you personally.

Once you've decided on your key priorities, where can you start to find out the answers to all your questions? The 'Resources' section at the end of this chapter lists publications and websites that collate this type of information. Using these as a first port of call can speed up your research no end, but there's no substitute for first-hand research at university/college open days and via their websites and prospectuses.

It is also well worth talking to former students from your school or college, family friends and older brothers and sisters about their experiences. More advice on this is given in the 'Researching your shortlist' section below.

> **TIP!**
>
> Don't forget to get university prospectuses (download or request a hard copy) and look at university/college websites.

Staying close to home?

A growing number of students only apply to universities and colleges that are within daily commuting distance – opting to save on living expenses while enjoying the support and comforts of home. With current tuition fees of up to £9,250, the choice of living in a hall of residence or in rented accommodation may not be affordable. But, don't forget, as mentioned in Chapter 3, in some towns where you might assume that living costs are high, rents can be lower than you think and it can be easy to find part-time jobs.

Studying from home could limit your 'student experience' though, as time spent travelling cuts down your opportunities for involvement in societies and social activities. You may also be less likely to network and make new friends, especially if you still have close friends from school living in the area. With the Covid-19 lockdowns, students' experiences of higher education have been considerably impacted, not least the social aspects.

You may decide on a compromise solution. A number of higher education courses – HNDs, Foundation degrees, even first degree courses – start with a year studying at a local, franchised further education college before transferring to the parent campus to complete your degree.

Researching your shortlist

As soon as you feel ready, draw up your shortlist of about 10 possible courses. From these you can select up to five final choices for your UCAS application. For each of your shortlist entries, make sure you've considered the following questions.

- What will I actually be studying on this course?
- Do I like the environment?
- Where's the course held? Many universities and colleges have several campuses. To avoid possible disappointment, research this now, as you wouldn't want to find yourself on a small satellite campus if you really wanted to be at the main site – or vice versa.
- Where will I live?
- Which options can I select on this course?
- How is progress assessed?
- Is there a tutorial system and how much support and advice on learning do students get?
- Can I achieve the qualifications needed for entry? (Chapter 6)

On the UCAS website you can find entries from individual universities and colleges. Most use the following format:

- Why study this course? Gives details on the topics studied and teaching and learning methods.
- Exchange possibilities with universities or colleges in other countries. Many institutions offer the opportunity to spend part of your course in another country – in Europe or much further afield – in the USA, Canada or Hong Kong for example. The list is almost endless.
- Location.
- Who is this course for?
- More about this course – description of individual modules, compulsory and optional, and any equipment needed.
- Modular structure.
- Skills and experience gained.
- After the course – information on careers entered by previous graduates.

It's important to attend open days and taster sessions at universities and colleges that really appeal to you, and to talk with student ambassadors who can answer your questions about university life. You can also arrange a visit to the department you're interested in; make sure to spend some time in the town or city as well in order to get some experience of the place where you might spend three or four years.

For students with disabilities, this is particularly important – you need to make sure the university or college will be able to meet your particular needs. Some campuses are better than others for wheelchairs, while some have special facilities for people who are visually impaired or deaf. Get in touch with the disability officers at your shortlisted universities or colleges. More information about access and facilities for students with disabilities is also available at ucas.com/disabled-students and, of course, from the prospectuses and websites of the universities and colleges themselves.

You should also attend UCAS events – real or virtual – to talk directly with representatives from higher education institutions about courses. They're free to attend but you'll need to book a place – either through school or college or individually. During the peak of the Covid-19 pandemic higher education institutions mostly ran virtual open events. While these can never properly replace a real visit, they can at least give some insight into the universities, their facilities and accommodation. Also, bear in mind that you could attend many more open events this way, allowing you to explore a wider range of institutions, courses and facilities more thoroughly. However, it's also important to get an experience of the locality, so it's wise to visit the area you intend studying in.

Read the details of the courses you're interested in and for which you think realistically that you can match the entry requirements. Highlight important points you may want to address in the personal statement part of your UCAS application, or refer to at interview.

TIPS!

Keep the prospectuses of places to which you're definitely applying!

Don't take anything as given. Email or phone departments directly and ask to speak to an admissions tutor if you want to ask specific questions, e.g. about the destinations of course graduates, possible career progression, admission details, or anything else. Tutors can be helpful and informative – they aren't there just to teach.

If you can't get to any open days, try watching the UCAS online virtual tours of different universities and colleges.

Selecting the final five

If there's one particular university or college you want to attend (perhaps because you're a mature student or can't move away from home), you can use your choices to apply for more than one course at the same institution (apart from at Oxford and Cambridge). On the other hand, at some universities or colleges it's not necessary to apply for more than one course because admission is to a faculty or group of related subjects.

The other major factor to consider in selecting your final five courses is the entry requirements. Most universities and colleges supply entry requirements for their courses at ucas.com. To maximise your chance of success, apply to courses that are likely to make you an offer – e.g. corresponding roughly with the grades you expect to achieve. This question is examined in greater detail in the next chapter.

Also, bear in mind you only get one UCAS personal statement, so if you choose to apply for different subjects be careful not to dilute the focus of your personal statement too much.

Chapter summary

University might well be your first experience of leaving home, so it is important to fully explore local amenities, availability of student accommodation, the student support available from the university or college, cost of living and the environment you will be living in, to ensure you'll feel happy in your new surroundings.

Resources

Publications

- *Heap 2023: University Degree Course Offers,* Trotman Education, www.trotman.co.uk.
- *The University Choice Journal,* Trotman, www.trotman.co.uk.

Websites

General

- www.applytouni.com.
- www.thecompleteuniversityguide.co.uk.
- www.discoveruni.gov.uk.
- www.theguardian.com/education/universityguide.
- https://indigo.careers.

- www.prospects.ac.uk.
- www.push.co.uk.
- www.sacu-student.com.
- www.studenthut.com.
- www.thestudentroom.co.uk.
- www.telegraph.co.uk/education/universities-colleges.
- www.ucas.com.
- www.ucas.com/open-days.
- www.ucas.com/taster-courses.
- www.ucas.com/virtual-tours.
- www.theuniguide.co.uk.
- www.whatuni.com.

For students with disabilities

- www.rnid.org.uk – Royal National Institute for Deaf People.
- www.disabilityrightsuk.org.
- www.rnib.org.uk – Royal National Institute of Blind People.

Case study - Josh

Josh decided to study mechanical engineering, but how did he decide which university to attend?

'I had always enjoyed and been good at physics and mathematics, so mechanical engineering was long in my sights as a university subject. The application of mathematics to solving real world solutions also attracted me to mechanical engineering; in that sense I had a head start in choosing what I was going to study at university.

'That said, I do think it is very important to choose the SUBJECT first, and then explore the universities where you could study. wanted to do a degree that gave me the option of an industrial placement as part of the course, so a sandwich degree in which I would spend my third year in a working environment was a big attraction. I used the discoveruni.gov.uk website to compare universities on employability of subjects, and my chosen university had a 95% success rate of mechanical engineering graduates being in graduate level employment within 6 months of completing their studies. This proved correct in my case, as I had two job offers with companies even before completing my degree, owing to the network of contacts I had built up while on placement.

'An important factor for me in my university choices was ease of transport between university sites as I have mobility difficulties.

I wanted to be sure that the universities were either campus based, thereby offering most facilities and access to lectures, etc on one site, or that the transport facilities between sites were good and frequent. My first-choice university when I came to accepting offers was the one that clearly offered the best support for students with additional needs. They were really helpful and always came back to me with clear answers to any questions or concerns I had.

'It is also very important to visit the university and the surrounding area, as you will be spending several years living there; you need to feel comfortable with the accommodation and facilities available. Virtual events are okay, but they can hide a lot; it is only by visiting a place for real that you will be able to get the real experience of all that it has to offer and whether it is right for you.'

6 | Academic requirements

You may have been thinking since Year 10 or 11 about whether you'll be able to meet higher education entry requirements, planning how your A levels, Scottish Highers, IB, ILC or BTEC Level 3 Awards will help you progress into higher education. Or you might not have given the matter any serious thought yet.

Either way, it's important to make sure you're realistic about the grades you hope to achieve, and that you target your applications to suitable universities and colleges.

This chapter will help you understand how they set their entry requirements and offers some basic dos and don'ts for choosing your final five courses.

What might the entry requirements be?

To enter higher education you normally need to achieve minimum qualifications equivalent to one of the following:

- two A levels
- one Double Award A level
- the Cambridge Pre-U
- one BTEC National Award
- two Advanced Highers
- an ILC
- an IB.

See pages 58–62 for a full list.

You'll also need:

- England – GCSEs at grades 9–4/5 or A*–C (including English language and Mathematics) depending on requirements at different institutions
- Scotland – National 5s at grades A*–C
- Wales and Northern Ireland – GCSEs at grades A*–C.

(Requirements vary for mature students and other groups – see page 81.)

In reality, most universities and colleges require more than the absolute minimum and many demand particular subjects for entry.

There are two main reasons for admission to some courses requiring higher than minimum grades.

1. **Coping with the course** – for the study of some subjects, a higher education department or faculty can decide their students need to achieve a particular qualification (say, B or C in A level Mathematics) in order to get through the course.
2. **Rationing places** – where there's high demand for a course the entry requirements will rise, because if a course asks for three Bs, fewer applicants will qualify for entry than if three Cs were requested (even though the three-C candidates might cope perfectly well with the course); these grade requirements help to prevent courses from becoming oversubscribed.

The second of these two reasons is the more common – so it's worth being aware that high grades are often an indication of popularity, and not always of quality. Some universities, colleges and courses are more popular than others and can therefore set high grades if they feel that the 'market' in a particular subject will bear them. It's worth knowing which courses are usually the most in demand.

On the equal-consideration deadline for applications, 26 January in 2022 (for 2022 entry), the top ten subject groups chosen by applicants were:

1. subjects allied to medicine (down 2%)
2. business and management studies (up 2%)
3. social sciences (down 3%)
4. creative arts and design (up 5%)
5. engineering and technology (up 1%)
6. biological and sport sciences (no change)
7. computing (up 13%)
8. psychology (up 5%)
9. law (up 4%)
10. medicine and dentistry (up 7%).

In addition, any course with a special feature (such as sponsorship or an exchange with a university or college overseas) can attract large numbers of applications and may therefore also require high grades.

Whatever course you apply for, your qualifications will be examined carefully by admissions tutors. They'll be looking at your advanced-level study and checking you have:

- the right subjects to satisfy entry requirements
- subjects they are prepared to include in an offer
- the types of qualification they want (e.g. A level, BTEC Extended Diploma)
- the right number of qualifications

- made an effort to fill any gaps in your record (e.g. by retaking GCSE mathematics at the same time as or before your advanced qualifications).

Admissions tutors will be on the lookout for students who are repeating advanced-level qualifications; your UCAS application must give full details of your results at the first attempt and include details of what you are repeating and when (see Chapter 15). Further explanations should be given in your personal statement.

Many admissions tutors will also attach a lot of importance to your results at GCSE or National 5 level. After all, these results, together with your predicted grades, will usually be the only evidence of your academic achievement to date. Tutors will be looking for:

- a reasonable spread of academic qualifications
- key subjects, like English language and mathematics (even if the university or college does not require them for your subject choice, most employers do)
- signs of academic capacity or potential.

Additional and alternative entry requirements

Applicants to music, art and design and other creative or performing arts courses often have to compile a portfolio of work, and may also have to attend an interview or audition (see Chapter 9).

If you'd like to train for work with young children or vulnerable adults (for example in teaching, social work or the healthcare professions), you'll need a criminal record check from one of the national disclosure and barring services, known as an Enhanced DBS check (see Chapter 24).

To study medicine, vaccinations for the following are required: measles, mumps, rubella, tuberculosis, diphtheria, tetanus, polio, meningitis and haemophilus influenzae b. At medical school it is likely that you will be given the hepatitis B vaccine. To study nursing, all nurses, but particularly those who work with infants, need tetanus, diphtheria, and pertussis vaccines. Other important immunisations include hepatitis B, varicella, measles, mumps, and rubella. Check the immunisation requirements with the universities and colleges you've chosen.

If you're applying for career-related courses, such as law or veterinary science, work experience may be an essential prerequisite for entry. Check this well before applying to give you time to gain any experience you need.

Students with certain disabilities may also be offered different entry requirements – it's worth checking with admissions tutors for individual courses as the criteria for admission may be relaxed.

How are entry requirements expressed?

Entry requirements may be expressed as specific grades (e.g. ABC at A level or ABBB at Scottish Higher), as a target number of UCAS Tariff points (e.g. 120 points) or as a mixture of the two (e.g. 120 points, including at least grade B in A level Chemistry).

The UCAS Tariff

The UCAS Tariff is the system for allocating points to the qualifications used for entry to higher education.

As if the number of qualifications available weren't confusing enough, different qualifications can have different grading structures (alphabetical, numerical or a mixture of both). Finding out what qualifications are needed for different higher education courses can be very confusing – the Tariff allows students to use a range of different qualifications to help secure a place on an undergraduate course.

Admission to higher education courses generally depends on an individual's achievement in level 3 qualifications, e.g. A levels or Scottish Highers. The UCAS Tariff gives a points value to each of these. Also included in the Tariff are a number of other qualifications that can be counted to boost the overall points score you're aiming to achieve.

Some universities and colleges use the UCAS Tariff to make comparisons between applicants with different qualifications. Tariff points are often used in entry requirements, although other factors are often taken into account as well. Entry details (available from UCAS and on the institutions' own websites) provide a fuller picture of what admissions tutors are seeking.

The tables on pages 58–62 show the points values for the most common qualifications covered by the UCAS Tariff. To see the points values for other qualifications you may hold or be studying for, you should visit www.ucas.com/tariff, and search for the qualification.

TIP!

If you have (or are likely to achieve) less than the minimum qualifications for entry to an honours degree course, your qualification level may be suitable for entry to an HND course or Foundation degree. You can then convert this additional qualification into a full degree with an additional year of study (see Chapter 4).

UCAS Tariff Points tables

A levels and AS

Grade					Tariff points
GCE & AVCE Double Award	A level with additional AS	GCE A level and AVCE	GCE AS Double Award	GCE AS & AS VCE	
A*A*					112
A*A					104
AA					96
AB					88
BB					80
	A*A				76
BC					72
	AA				68
CC	AB				64
CD	BB	A*			56
	BC				52
DD		A			48
	CC				44
	CD				42
DE		B	AA		40
			AB		36
	DD				34
EE		C	BB		32
	DE				30
			BC		28
		D	CC		24
	EE		CD		22
			DD	A	20
		E	DE	B	16
			EE	C	12
				D	10
				E	6

TIP!

Entry requirements are listed on each course listing in the UCAS search tool. Check these before you apply and keep an eye on them, as requirements are subject to change!

Scottish Highers/Advanced Highers

Grade	Higher	Advanced Higher
A	33	56
B	27	48
C	21	40
D	15	32

Advanced Welsh Baccalaureate – Skills Challenge Certificate

Grade	Tariff points
A*	56
A	48
B	40
C	32
D	24
E	16

Irish Leaving Certificate

Grade Higher	Ordinary	Tariff points
A1		36
A2		30
B1		30
B2		24
B3		24
C1		18
C2		18
C3	A1	12
D1		12
	A2	10
	B1	10
D2		9
D3		9
	B2	8
	B3	8
	C1	6
	C2	6

International Baccalaureate (IB) Diploma

While the IB Diploma does not attract UCAS Tariff points, the individual qualifications within the IB Diploma do, so the total Tariff points for an IB Diploma can be calculated by adding together each of the following four components:

IB Certificate in Higher Level

Grade	Tariff points
H7	56
H6	48
H5	32
H4	24
H3	12
H2	0
H1	0

Size band: 4
Grade bands: 3–14

IB Certificate in Standard Level

Grade	Tariff points
S7	28
S6	24
S5	16
S4	12
S3	6
S2	0
S1	0

Size band: 2
Grade bands: 3–14

IB Certificate in Extended Essay

Grade	Tariff points
A	12
B	10
C	8
D	6
E	4

Size band: 1
Grade bands: 4–12

IB Certificate in Theory of Knowledge

Grade	Tariff points
A	12
B	10
C	8
D	6
E	4

Size band: 1
Grade bands: 4–12
Certificates in Extended Essay and Theory of Knowledge are awarded Tariff points when the certificates have been taken individually.

Cambridge International Pre-U Certificate

Grade	Principal Subject	Global Perspective and Research	Short Course
D1	56	56	22
D2	56	56	20
D3	52	52	20
M1	44	44	18
M2	40	40	14
M3	36	36	12
P1	28	28	10
P2	24	24	8
P3	20	20	6

Progression Diploma

Grade	Tariff points
A*	168
A	144
B	120
C	96
D	72
E	48

Extended Project – Stand alone

Grade	Tariff points
A*	28
A	24
B	20
C	16
D	12
E	8

Music examinations

Performance			Theory			Tariff points
Grade 8	Grade 7	Grade 6	Grade 8	Grade 7	Grade 6	
D						30
M						24
P						18
	D					16
	M	D				12
	P	M	D			10
			M			9
			P	D		8
				M		7
		P		P	D	6
					M	5
					P	4

Additional points will be awarded for music examinations from the Associated Board of the Royal Schools of Music (ABRSM), University of West London, Rockschool and Trinity Guildhall/Trinity College London (music examinations at grades 6, 7, 8 (D=Distinction; M=Merit; P=Pass)).

NB: Full acknowledgement is made to UCAS for this information. For further details of all qualifications awarded UCAS Tariff points see ucas.com/tariff. Note that new qualifications are introduced each year.

Further information on the Tariff

Although Tariff points can be accumulated in a variety of ways, not all of these will necessarily be acceptable for entry to a particular higher education course. So, the achievement of a points score doesn't give you an automatic right to a place, and admissions staff take many other factors into account when selecting students. The UCAS search tool at www.ucas.com is the best source of reference for which qualifications are acceptable for entry to specific courses.

How does the Tariff work?

- Students can collect Tariff points from a range of different qualifications.
- There's no ceiling to the number of points that can be accumulated.
- There's no double counting. Certain qualifications in the Tariff build on qualifications in the same subject that also attract Tariff points. Tariff points are generally only counted for the highest level of achievement in a subject. This means you can't usually count AS grades if you have an A level in the same subject and you can't count a BTEC Diploma if you have the Extended Diploma in the same subject.

- UCAS Tariff points are allocated to Level 3/SCQF Level 6 qualifications.
- Where the Tariff refers to specific awarding bodies, only qualifications from these awarding bodies attract Tariff points.
- Qualifications with a similar title but from a different awarding body don't attract Tariff points.

How does higher education use the Tariff?

Not all qualifications attract UCAS Tariff points. The universities or colleges you're interested in may accept your qualifications anyway.

Not all institutions use the UCAS Tariff. Some prefer to express their entry requirements and make offers in terms of qualifications and grades rather than in Tariff points. Around one-third of course entry requirements make reference to the Tariff.

The courses that refer to UCAS Tariff points in their entry requirements do so in different ways:

- some list their entry requirements and make offers using only Tariff points, with no reference to specific qualifications or grades
- some ask for specific qualifications and a set number of Tariff points
- some link the Tariff points required to specific qualifications and grades. Examples include:
  - o   120 points to include a grade B in A level History
  - o   120 points including SQA Higher grade B in Mathematics
  - o   120 points. A levels, Scottish Highers and BTEC National Diplomas are acceptable qualifications
  - o   120 points. Points from General Studies A level, AS exams, key skills and COPE won't be considered
  - o   120 points gained from at least three A levels or equivalent 18 unit qualifications
  - o   120 points including A level Mathematics and Physics.

Use of the Tariff may also vary from department to department at any one university or college, and may in some cases depend on the programme being offered.

Unit grade information

There is space for you to fill in your unit grade scores on your UCAS application – but you don't have to do so. (See under **Which qualifications should I add?** in Chapter 15.) Unit grades may be specified as part of conditional offers, but this practice is not widespread.

You should look at individual university and college prospectuses and websites to check entry requirements and profiles to find out their individual policies on unit grade information.

Subjects

It's important to check the combination of advanced-level subjects that's acceptable for admission to particular courses. This can sometimes be quite specific! Some departments, particularly at some of the UK's older universities, prefer the more traditional A level, Scottish Higher and IB subjects for the minimum entry requirement to some courses.

The list below shows the most commonly approved subjects:

- biology
- chemistry
- classical civilisation
- classical languages
- computing
- drama and theatre studies
- economics
- English (English language, English literature, and English language and literature)
- environmental science
- further mathematics
- geography
- geology
- government & politics
- history
- history of art
- law
- mathematics
- modern languages
- music
- philosophy
- physics
- psychology
- religious studies
- sociology
- statistics.

However, if you have taken subjects that aren't on the above list, they may still be acceptable for university entry. From 2015 to 2018 some subjects were removed under government reforms of the A level qualification and are no longer available. As a rule of thumb, subjects that may have overlapping content, such as business studies and economics or geography and environmental science, are acceptable individually but as a pair are less likely to be acceptable.

In May 2019 the Russell Group of 24 universities announced that it was scrapping its list of 'preferred' A level subjects. The list was originally drawn up to help pupils make informed decisions about their path to further education. However, critics say it sidelined subjects such as art, music and drama, which was detrimental to the creative industries.

The Russell Group insists the list was never intended to be a set of hard-and-fast requirements. On its website, it said: 'We have sometimes heard other people suggest that facilitating subjects are the only subjects pupils should consider to get into a Russell Group university, or that you must take them for any degree. This has never been the case.'

As an alternative, the Russell Group has launched the Informed Choices website (www.informedchoices.ac.uk), which allows students to explore various degrees and subject areas they are interested in.

Generally speaking, if you're taking two or more of the following subjects (and related titles) at advanced level, even though each one may be approved individually, you should check that the combination will be acceptable for entry to the higher education courses you're considering:

- accounting
- art
- dance
- design and technology
- drama
- environmental science
- film studies
- media studies
- music technology
- photography
- physical education.

The following courses are no longer available at A level, but can be taken as an A-level equivalent vocational qualification, e.g. BTEC Subsidiary Diploma:

- health & social care
- leisure studies
- performing arts
- sports studies.

For some specialised career-related higher-education courses, two or more subjects from the upper above list would be useful. However, a common misconception among students, and for that matter, parents, is that all subjects should be relevant to the chosen university course. This isn't the case – universities are often more interested in the skillset students bring, e.g. a modern foreign language is an advantage for entry to business-based degrees, as are sciences or mathematics as they develop analytical skills, along with humanities subjects such as history as they develop written communication and research skills.

So, it really is essential to check the exact entry requirements for any course you are considering. There are no standard university-wide lists available, so the only way to clarify this is by consulting the admissions requirements for the course you'd like to study.

Targeting the right courses

Here are a few dos and don'ts to make sure that your chosen final five courses give you the best chance of success.

Do ...

- Read course descriptions very carefully. Remember that courses with similar titles can have very different content, which can also affect the subjects required for entry.
- Carefully check the required entry grades and qualifications on the UCAS website, then confirm them by checking the university or college prospectuses or websites. If you are unsure on any point contact the institutions directly to make sure there's no chance you have misunderstood or to ask whether any changes have been made since the information was written.
- Check that the post-16 qualifications you've opted to take will give you the entry qualifications you need, and check with your subject teachers that you're on track to achieve the right grades.
- Be realistic about the grades you're likely to achieve. Make sure that you know what exam grades teachers are going to predict for you.
- As a safety net, make sure you apply to at least one course that's likely to give you a slightly lower offer. However, if at all possible, only add a university/course that you'd genuinely be prepared to take.

Don't ...

- Apply for lots of different or unrelated subjects – you'll have a difficult job justifying this in your personal statement, and admissions tutors will question how genuine your interest is in each subject.
- Even if you expect high grades, think very carefully before applying to five very popular universities for a very popular subject. Entry will be extremely competitive and, even with high predicted grades, you can't be sure of being accepted. Better to include at least one university or college that is not so oversubscribed, and therefore makes offers at a slightly lower level.

Chapter summary

Be positive, but realistic, in your higher education applications. And have a backup plan! As you'll see in Part II, you'll have the opportunity to make a first (Firm) choice and a backup (Insurance) choice in response to university or college offers on your UCAS application – make sure your backup choice is on a course and in a place you'll genuinely enjoy.

Resources

Publications

- *Choose the Right A Levels: The A–Z Guide*, Trotman Education, www.trotman.co.uk.
- *Heap 2023: University Degree Course Offers,* Trotman Education, www.trotman.co.uk.

Websites

- www.gov.uk/government/organisations/disclosure-and-barring-service – criminal records check in England and Wales.
- www.justice-ni.gov.uk – criminal records check in Northern Ireland.
- www.mygov.scot/basic-disclosure/apply-for-basic-disclosure – criminal records check in Scotland.
- www.push.co.uk.
- www.telegraph.co.uk/education/universities-colleges.
- www.thecompleteuniversityguide.co.uk.
- www.theguardian.com/education/universityguide.
- www.timeshighereducation.com.
- www.ucas.com.

Part II
The admissions procedure: applications, interviews, offers and beyond

7 | Applications and offers

Making your application

As the timetable on pages 3–6 shows, if you're on a two-year advanced course, ideally you should do all your higher education research work by September or October of the second year – more than a year before you start in higher education.

If you're on a one-year course, you won't have time to do all the activities suggested for the first year, but you'll be working to the same application deadlines so you still need to research all your options.

UCAS applicant journey

The UCAS applicant journey (see Figure 1, page 71) has been designed to guide you through the different steps you will take when making your application for higher education.

Deadlines

There are two deadlines for applications to courses through UCAS. They are 18:00 hours (UK time) on 15 October and 25 January.

The deadline for application to most courses is 18:00 hours (UK time), 25 January. (Remember, however, that you will have to submit your application to your referee well before this to make sure it reaches UCAS in time.) All applications submitted by 25 January are considered – however, it's advisable to apply as early as you can.

Aim to submit your UCAS application to your referee by late November or by any internal deadline given by your school or college. You're still able to apply after 25 January and universities and colleges may consider your application if they still have places – but they are not obliged to do so. Any applications received after 30 June will be referred to Clearing (see Chapter 10). However, if you are applying as an international student you may apply until 30 June without being regarded as a late applicant.

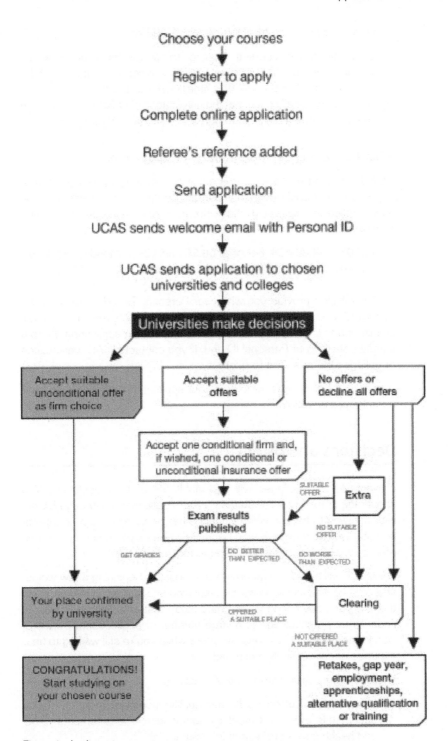

Figure 1: Applicant journey

Some courses have an earlier application deadline:

● applications for courses leading to professional qualifications in medicine, dentistry or veterinary science/medicine must be submitted by 18:00 hours (UK time) on 15 October

● applications for all courses at the universities of Oxford or Cambridge must be submitted by 18:00 hours (UK time) on 15 October.

What happens once you submit your application?

UCAS will send you a welcome email acknowledging receipt of your application and confirming your personal details and the courses you have applied for. You must check that this information is correct, and contact UCAS immediately if it isn't:

● call 0371 4680 468, between 08:30 and 18:00, Monday to Friday
● call +44 330 3330 230 from outside the UK.

UCAS will also provide you with your Personal ID and, along with the password you used for your application (see Chapter 11), this will enable you to log in and follow the progress of your application. Keep a careful note of your Personal ID and, if you contact UCAS, universities or colleges, be prepared to quote it.

Admissions tutors can now look at your application and decide whether to make you an offer.

Decisions and offers

Universities and colleges will inform UCAS of their decisions. You should log in to check the status of your application – although UCAS will email you to tell you when a change has been made to your application status. The message won't specify whether you have received an offer or a rejection, but will ask you to log in to find out.

Decisions will arrive in a random order, possibly beginning a few weeks after you apply. Decisions will be displayed as soon as UCAS receives them. If you have a long wait, it may mean that an admissions tutor is under great pressure due to a large number of applications. So, don't worry if people you know receive offers while you're still waiting to hear – it does not necessarily mean bad news.

There are three main categories of decision.

1. **Unconditional offer**: no further qualifications are required. If you accept this offer, and meet all non-academic requirements (DBS and health checks for example), you are in!
2. **Conditional offer**: you still have some work to do ... but if you accept the offer and achieve the conditions in the examinations you are about to take, a place will be guaranteed.

3. **Unsuccessful**: sorry – no luck. However, it may be that you receive an offer from one of your other choices. If all decisions are unsuccessful, you shouldn't feel discouraged, as there's still the option of applying to courses through UCAS Extra and, later in the application cycle, Clearing.

The following decisions may also appear:

- withdrawn: you have withdrawn this choice
- cancelled: you have asked UCAS to cancel this choice.

Universities and colleges have to decide by 18 May whether to offer you a place, provided you applied by the deadline of 25 January.

Interviews and open days

Before they make a decision, admissions tutors may invite you to an interview. Be prepared to travel to universities or colleges during the late autumn and winter – a 16–25 Railcard or a National Express Young Persons Coachcard might be a good investment! Since the start of the Covid-19 pandemic in 2020, universities have increasingly been conducting interviews virtually using online platforms.

Some universities and colleges will contact you directly to invite you for interview. Others will inform you of interview details through your UCAS application. If you're invited for interview through UCAS, you'll receive an email asking you to look at the change to your application. You can accept the interview invitation, decline it or request an alternative date or time.

If you need to change the interview time or date, you should also contact the university or college direct. They can then update the invitation so that the revised details are shown on your UCAS application. You should try to attend interviews on the first date given, as it may be difficult for admissions tutors to offer an alternative date.

Advice on preparing for interviews is given in Chapter 9.

Alternatively, you may be offered a conditional or unconditional place and invited to attend an open day. You might also be asked to submit a portfolio or piece of written work.

Replying to offers

You will be asked to reply to any offers you receive – and you must do so – but you don't have to reply until you have received decisions from all the universities and colleges to which you applied. UCAS will give you a deadline for replying. This may be different from the deadlines received by your friends. Don't worry about this. There's no one single deadline – UCAS acts only after you have heard from all your choices.

Through your UCAS application, you must reply to each offer with one of three options.

1. **Firm acceptance**. If you firmly accept an offer (either as an unconditional offer or as a conditional offer), this means you're sure that this offer is your first preference of all the offers you've received through UCAS. If you get the grades, this will be the higher education course you take. You can make this reply only once – you won't be able to change or cancel your reply. There's also an equal commitment on the university's or college's part to accept you if you fulfil the conditions.
2. **Insurance acceptance**. If you've firmly accepted a conditional offer, you may also hold one additional offer (either conditional or unconditional) as an insurance acceptance. This is your fall-back, in case your grades are too low for your firm acceptance. It's worth knowing you're not obliged to make an insurance reply – if you do so and then your firm acceptance offer isn't confirmed, you'll be expected to attend your insurance choice if that's confirmed. If you don't feel 100% committed to your insurance choice, it would be better to wait and see what is available in Clearing. Please ask for advice before making this decision!
3. **Decline**. If you decline an offer, you're indicating that you definitely don't wish to accept it.

You must either accept or decline your offers. You can accept two offers (your firm and insurance choices) and must decline all your other offers, so your combination of replies will be one of the following:

- accept one offer firmly (unconditional firm or conditional firm) and decline any others
- accept one offer firmly (conditional firm) and one as an insurance (unconditional insurance or conditional insurance), and decline any others
- decline all offers.

If you firmly accept an **unconditional** offer of a place, you're not entitled to choose an insurance offer. If you firmly accept a **conditional** offer, you may accept an unconditional offer or another conditional offer as your insurance acceptance.

> **TIP!**
>
> Don't worry if people you know receive replies before you do. This does not mean that you are going to be rejected. Some admissions tutors, for various reasons, take longer to deal with applications than others.

Tips on making your replies

- Consider your replies very carefully. Ask for advice from your school/college tutor or careers adviser.
- Don't accept an offer (firm or insurance) unless you're sure that you will be happy to enrol on the course.
- It's advisable to choose an unconditional offer as your insurance acceptance or one with conditions that are easier for you to meet than those of your firm acceptance.
- Don't include as an insurance acceptance a course that you would be unwilling to take up. If you're not accepted for your firm choice and the insurance offer is confirmed, you're committed to going there. It would be better not to hold an insurance acceptance than to hold one you wouldn't be willing to take up.
- Bear in mind the precise requirements of the offer. For example, if a BCC offer requires a B in a subject you're not very confident about, but an offer requiring higher grades overall doesn't specify the B in that subject or perhaps counts general studies, then your firm/insurance decision needs to take these factors into account.

What if you don't get any offers?

If you're in this position, you may be able to make a further application in Extra between 23 February and 4 July. In 2021, 5,255 people were placed through Extra.

You'll be eligible to use Extra if you've used all five choices in your original application and you fulfil any one of the following criteria:

- you've had unsuccessful or withdrawn decisions for all your choices
- you've cancelled your outstanding choices and hold no offers
- you've received decisions from all five choices and have declined all offers made to you.

> **TIP!**
>
> If you applied to only one course and you haven't accepted or declined your offers, you have the option of adding more choices through your UCAS application before 30 June. You'll have to pay the additional £4.50 application fee.

If you're eligible to use Extra, UCAS will let you know. When you log in to your UCAS application, you'll see the option to 'Add choice'. You'll still be able to search for courses that have vacancies in the UCAS search tool on the website. You can apply for several courses – but only one at a time.

> **TIP!**
>
> It is a good idea to contact the admissions tutors for the courses that interest you and ask whether they will consider you.

When you enter the Extra course details on your UCAS application, it is automatically sent online to the relevant university or college.

If you're made an offer, you can then choose whether to accept it. If you're currently studying for examinations, any offer that you receive is likely to be a conditional one and will contain the required exam grades. If you decide to accept a conditional offer, you won't be able to take any further part in Extra. (There are no insurance options in Extra.) If you already have your exam results, you may receive an unconditional offer. Once you accept an unconditional offer, you have that place.

If you're unsuccessful, decline an offer or do not receive an offer **within 21 days of choosing a course** through Extra, you can (time permitting) make a further application in Extra. The Extra button on your Track screen will be reactivated.

Tips on using Extra

- Do some careful research and seek guidance from your school, college or careers adviser and from the universities and colleges themselves.
- Think very carefully before applying again for the types of course for which you have already been unsuccessful – it may simply result in another rejection.
- Be flexible – for example, if you applied to high-demand courses and universities and colleges in your original application and were unsuccessful, you could consider related or alternative subjects.
- If you're not offered a place in Extra, you may still find a place through Clearing (see Chapter 10).
- You can find out more about Extra on the UCAS website, at ucas.com/extra.

8 | Non-standard applications

Applications for the majority of courses follow the pattern outlined in the previous chapters. However, there are some exceptions, specifically for:

- courses at the universities of Oxford and Cambridge
- music conservatoires
- medicine, dentistry and veterinary science or veterinary medicine courses
- mature students
- deferred entry
- late applications
- international students.

Oxford and Cambridge

If you intend to apply for any course at either Oxford or Cambridge, the deadline for submitting your application is 18:00 hours (UK time) on 15 October 2022. (Additional forms must be submitted at an earlier date if you want to be considered for a music or choral scholarship at either university. You can find details on their websites.)

All Cambridge University colleges will accept mature students, but three are exclusively for mature students: Hughes Hall, St Edmund's College and Wolfson College.

Shortly after submitting your UCAS application, you'll be asked via email to complete an online Supplementary Application Questionnaire (SAQ). You must submit your SAQ by the deadline set. In the majority of cases this deadline will be 18:00 hours (UK time) on 22 October 2022.

The purpose of the SAQ, Cambridge says, is to ensure that admissions tutors have consistent information about all applicants. It also permits them to collect information that is not part of the UCAS application such as the topics students have covered as part of A level (or equivalent) courses and helps the interviewers decide which questions to ask.

Cambridge interviews are conducted in certain countries (Canada, China, Hong Kong, India, Malaysia and Singapore). If you want to take advantage of this scheme, rather than come to Cambridge, you must consult the list of dates on the website. However, applicants invited for interview for architecture, history of art, classics and music are advised to travel to Cambridge for interview.

Most applicants to the University of Oxford are not required to submit a separate form, but extra information is required for some international interviews, and choral and organ award applicants must submit an additional form online by 1 September 2022.

You can apply to only one course at *either* the University of Oxford or the University of Cambridge. *You cannot apply to both universities.* There is only one exception to this – if you'll be a graduate at the start of the course and you're applying for course code A101 (graduate medicine) at the University of Cambridge, you can also apply to medicine (course code A100) at Cambridge and graduate medicine (course code A101) at the University of Oxford. No other combinations are permitted. However, those applying for organ awards can audition at both universities.

Some applicants will need to complete an additional application form. For full information about applying to the universities of Oxford or Cambridge, please visit their websites at www.ox.ac.uk or www.study. cam.ac.uk. In-depth advice on making applications to these universities is also given in *Getting into Oxford & Cambridge* (Trotman Education).

Applying to study at a conservatoire

You can apply for performance-based music, dance, drama and musical theatre courses at nine of the UK conservatoires online using the UCAS Conservatoires scheme, which is run by UCAS and works in a similar way. You can select six courses rather than the five possible through the UCAS Undergraduate scheme. The application fee for UCAS Conservatoires is £27 and there are also audition fees to pay.

The nine conservatoires are:

1. Bristol Old Vic Theatre School
2. Leeds College of Music (undergraduate courses through UCAS and postgraduate course through UCAS Conservatoires)
3. Royal Academy of Music
4. Royal Birmingham Conservatoire
5. Royal College of Music
6. Royal Conservatoire of Scotland
7. Royal Northern College of Music
8. Royal Welsh College of Music and Drama
9. Trinity Laban Conservatoire of Music and Dance.

If you're applying for music courses, you can choose either a joint course (50/50), a major/minor course (75/25) or you can provide two options, either of which you'd be happy to study.

You can apply for music, dance, drama and musical theatre courses from 15 July 2022. For music courses the application deadline is 18:00 hours (UK time) on 3 October 2022, although late entries may be considered if there are vacancies.

For most undergraduate dance, drama and musical theatre courses the deadline is 25 January 2023. There are some exceptions though – particularly for certain audition locations and for international applicants – so it's important to check the conservatoire websites for full details.

Applying to UCAS Conservatoires doesn't mean you're excluded from the UCAS Undergraduate system. The two systems run independently, so you can also make up to five choices through UCAS Undergraduate. However, you may only accept a place through one of the systems.

Some members of the organisation Conservatoires UK don't recruit through UCAS Conservatoires. They use either the standard UCAS scheme or run their own independent admissions systems. They include:

- some of the colleges that are part of the group Conservatoire for Dance and Drama
- Guildhall School of Music and Drama
- Royal Central School of Speech and Drama.

Conservatoire auditions preparation advice from Nicola Peacock of the Royal College of Music

Auditions are a busy time for conservatoire staff, but also exciting, as we get to meet the talented new students who will be joining us next year. We are very aware that auditioning at a conservatoire can seem a daunting prospect, but we really want applicants to have a positive experience and a lot of effort goes into ensuring we look after you on the day.

How to prepare
Each conservatoire will have information on its website about what you need to prepare and any particular requirements, so check these carefully when you know your audition date. If you don't understand something, please don't be afraid to contact us to ask.

Practical tips
Our top tip would be to allow plenty of time for your journey, so that you arrive on time feeling calm and prepared. There is no need to wear concert dress – we would recommend smart casual clothes that you feel comfortable in. Don't forget to bring along the music for both you and your accompanist (people really do forget!) and anything you may need for your instrument, like spare reeds, strings, or a mute.

When you arrive, there will be people on hand to direct you to your audition room and answer any last minute questions. Audition stewards are often current students, so take the opportunity to ask them what student life is like!

For performers auditioning in the UK, the conservatoire can usually provide an accompanist for you, and you will have time to warm up together before the audition.

The audition

The exact structure of your audition will depend on the conservatoire and your specialism, but for most instrumental and vocal performers, your audition will probably last around 15–20 minutes. There will normally be two or three panellists, who will be experts in your specialism. They may choose which of your pieces they want to hear, and don't worry if they don't ask you to play all the way to the end of what you prepared. There will probably also be a sight-reading test and some auditions may include some scales or aural work. It is possible you may also get asked to perform for a second panel or in a group workshop. For composers, your portfolio will have already been assessed, so the panel will want to talk to you about your ideas in more detail. There may be some different assessments too for students of dance and drama, such as dance classes or a group interview.

Ask questions

Most auditions will include a conversation about your experience and interests. Don't forget that this is a chance for you to get a feel for the conservatoire and ask us some questions! You might want to ask about performance opportunities on the programme, or which professors you could end up working with.

Good luck!

If you have any questions about your conservatoire application, check out our website – www.rcm.ac.uk – or send us a message on Facebook (www.facebook.com/royalcollegeofmusic) or Twitter (@RCMLondon).

Medicine, dentistry and veterinary science/veterinary medicine courses

If you want to apply for a course leading to a professional qualification in medicine, dentistry or veterinary science/medicine, the deadline for submitting your application is 18:00 hours (UK time) on 15 October 2022. You're allowed to select a maximum of four courses in any one of these subjects – if you list more than four, your UCAS application (described fully in Part III) will ask you to reduce your number of choices. You can, if you'd like to, use the remaining space on your UCAS application for a course in another subject. There's strong competition for entry to these professional courses and many people are disappointed in their first choice of study.

In-depth advice on making applications in these subject areas is given in the *Getting into* series (see the 'Resources' section at the end of this chapter).

Mature students

There's no single definition of a 'mature' applicant, but most universities and colleges now classify students as 'mature' if they are over 21 years of age at the date of entry to a course. The vast majority of departments welcome applications from mature students, and many, especially science departments, would like more.

As a mature student, you're more likely to be accepted with qualifications that wouldn't be good enough if they were presented by a student aged 18 in full-time education. That said, there's still fierce competition for places, and in most subjects places aren't set aside for mature students. If you're considered favourably, you're likely to be called for interview. It isn't usually advisable to rely only on qualifications gained several years ago at school; university and college departments will probably want to see recent evidence of your academic ability so that they can evaluate your application fairly. In addition, taking a course of study at the right level helps prepare you for full-time student life.

The Access to Higher Education Diploma, for example, is for students aged 19 or over who do not hold the formal qualifications required for university entry. It provides excellent preparation for study at higher education level. Access Diplomas vary in subject emphasis, and what is available depends on your locality. Access courses are often linked to particular higher education courses at certain institutions.

It's also very important to demonstrate relevant work experience if you're applying for courses leading to any of the caring professions or those related to medicine.

Admissions tutors for courses you're interested in will be able to advise you. If they do expect evidence of recent study they might suggest:

- attending a further education college to study for one of the usual post-16 qualifications (e.g. an A level, Higher or National Award)
- taking one of the Access to Higher Education or Foundation courses specially designed for mature students.

You may also find that, through what's known as **Accreditation of Prior Learning** (APL), you can gain acceptance of alternative qualifications or, through **Accreditation of Prior Experiential Learning** (APEL), acceptance of some of the skills you have developed in the workplace. You'll need to contact universities and colleges direct to find out what their policies are.

Definitions:

- Accreditation of Prior Learning (APL, also known as Recognition of Prior Learning) is essentially credit awarded for wider learning gained through self-directed study, work or training. It's a process used by many organisations around the world, including higher education institutions, to evaluate skills and knowledge acquired outside formal education. Methods of assessing prior learning are varied and include: evaluation of experience gained through volunteer work, previous paid or unpaid employment, or observation of actual workplace behaviour.
- Accreditation of Prior Experiential Learning (APEL) is an extension of APL that includes assessed learning gained from life and work experience. APEL is similar to APL in that it's recognition of prior learning but is broader as in theory it allows for learning from any prior experience. Often APEL and APL are used synonymously and the terms overlap.

For further information visit www.ucas.com/mature-students.

> **TIPS!**
>
> Evidence of relevant work experience will boost your application and show that you know what you're committing to.
>
> Evidence of previous study will show that you'll be able to cope with the academic content of the course.
>
> It's advisable for mature students to contact departments directly to ask about their admissions policies before applying to UCAS and to tailor their applications accordingly.

Deferred entry

Taking a gap year is an increasingly popular option for many students – offering a unique opportunity to broaden horizons, travel or work as a volunteer. And, as the cost of higher education continues to rise, it can be a good way to save some money while gaining valuable experience in the workplace. If you do plan, for whatever reason, to defer your entry into higher education until 2024, there are three options available to you – each is listed below with a few notes on the pros and cons.

Option 1: apply through UCAS for deferred entry

You can make your application this year and select a start date of 2024 in your UCAS application to show you want to defer your entry (see Chapter 24). The major advantage of this option is that you get the formalities out of the way while you're still at school or college and available for interview – then you can relax. It's important to note that you'll still have to meet the terms of offers made to you.

Generally speaking, applications for deferred entry are dealt with in the normal way, but for some subjects (such as medicine, certain science and mathematics subjects and professional subjects) admissions tutors may be a little cautious about offering you a place. (They may say they want to be sure that your skills and knowledge are really up to date.) So it's important you're sure you want to defer, and to check with the department you're applying to whether they would be happy to admit you a year later.

Remember, if you do apply for entry in 2024 but then find that you have no useful way of spending the gap year after all, the university or college is not obliged to take you a year earlier (i.e. in 2023). If you choose to defer, remember to mention your reasons and plans for your year out in the personal statement section of your UCAS application (see Chapter 23); this is much more likely to make admissions tutors willing to give you a deferred place.

Option 2: apply through UCAS for standard entry

If you're not confident enough of your decision to apply for deferred entry on your UCAS application, you can apply for the normal admission year and, later on, ask the university or college where you're accepted whether you can defer. This means you don't need to say anything on your UCAS application about deferred entry. However, the university or college is quite entitled to say that the place it has offered you is for 2023 entry only, and you could either take it up or start a new application for entry in 2024.

Option 3: don't apply through UCAS until the following year

It's possible to delay applying to UCAS until after you've received your results – making your UCAS application during your gap year. This can be a good option in some instances, especially if your exam results turn out to be significantly different from those that were predicted. Your grades are also guaranteed, and if you accept an offer it will be a firm decision, so universities and colleges may consider you a better bet than a candidate who is only predicted those grades. The disadvantage, though, is that you must find time during your gap year to get your research up to date, fill in your UCAS application and (possibly) attend open days and interviews. This can limit your gap year options as you'll need to be contactable at all times. Flying back from Australia (or anywhere you might decide to spend your gap year) to attend an interview could put a serious dent in your finances!

Making a late application

If at all possible, avoid applying late. Many popular courses fill up quickly, and getting a place will be more difficult, if not impossible. However, if you decide you'd like to apply to higher education late, you still can. Up to 30 June, UCAS will send your application to your named institutions, but the universities and colleges will only consider you at their discretion. If they do choose to consider you, the same procedures are followed as for a normal application, and you'll reply to offers in the usual way. Applications received between 1 July and 21 September will be processed through the Clearing scheme, which operates from 5 July to late October.

International students

If you're an international student, the general information given in this chapter and Chapter 7 applies to you. However, UCAS has some specific additional advice for you.

- Make sure you add all the qualifications you have or are currently working for. Visit ucas.com/fillinginyourapplication for advice on entering qualifications on your application.
- Give as much information as possible – without it, admissions tutors will struggle to make a decision.
- You may have to send proof of your results in certificates or transcripts to the universities or colleges. They all have different policies on how they want to receive them. While some of them ask you to send everything straight away, others will do their initial assessment of your application before asking to see proof of your results.
- Although UCAS can send some results from the awarding bodies to your chosen universities and colleges – including the International Baccalaureate – for most international qualifications you'll have to send them direct to universities and colleges yourself.
- Follow the advice in Chapter 21 for your personal statement, but also say why you want to study in the UK and describe your English language skills (mentioning any English courses or tests you have taken). Also explain why you want to be an international student rather than studying in your own country.

As mentioned in Chapter 7, your deadline for application is 30 June (although you are advised to apply as early as possible) but for courses listed on page 72 you must observe the same (earlier) deadlines as

UK students. You'll find a lot of useful information on ucas.com on costs of study here, visas and student life in the UK.

Visa requirements

Since 5 October 2020, students from outside the UK who need a visa to study at UK universities and colleges will apply for a Student visa. All international students on degree courses, including those from EU and EEA countries, need to apply through the Student visa route. This includes those from Europe coming to the UK to study.

To obtain a visa, the university that has made you an offer will need to act as a sponsor for your visa application. Once you have accepted the offer, the university will then give you a Confirmation of Acceptance for Studies (CAS) letter, after which you can apply for the visa.

You can apply for a Student visa either online at the www.gov.uk website or at a visa application centre local to you.

You need to show that you have:

- an offer of a place at a university or college
- the right level of English to join that course (see below)
- finances to pay for your first year of tuition fees and living expenses.

You can apply for a student visa from three months before the start date of your course if you are already in the UK, and from six months if you are outside the UK.

If you are already in the UK and eligible to apply for your student visa without returning to your home country, you must make sure there are no more than 28 days between the end of your previous course of study and the start of your new course. A standard Student visa application costs £348 if you apply from outside the UK, and £475 if you apply when you are already in the UK.

For full guidance on the requirements of student visa applications in relation to your circumstances, visit www.gov.uk/study-uk-student-visa and www.ukcisa.org.uk.

Resources

Publications

- *Getting into Art & Design Courses*, Trotman Education, www.trotman.co.uk.
- *Getting into Dental School*, Trotman Education, www.trotman.co.uk.
- *Getting into Medical School 2023 Entry*, Trotman Education, www.trotman.co.uk.

- *Getting into Oxford & Cambridge 2023 Entry*, Trotman Education, www.trotman.co.uk.
- *Getting into Veterinary School*, Trotman Education, www.trotman.co.uk.
- *Heap 2023: University Degree Course Offers,* Trotman Education, www.trotman.co.uk.

Websites

- www.cam.ac.uk: for information on applications to Cambridge.
- www.ox.ac.uk: for information on applications to Oxford.
- www.ucas.com/conservatoires.
- www.ucas.com/international-toolkit: includes a guide to applying to study in the UK in six different languages – Arabic, Chinese, French, German, Italian and Spanish.
- www.ucas.com/trackyourapplication: to find out what happens after you apply.

9 | Interviews and selection

In many cases, the decision to offer you a place will be made using the information you supplied on your application, but admissions tutors for several courses often require more detailed information about applicants. So you may be asked to attend an interview or audition, or to take a written test.

Interviews

Many universities and colleges (especially the popular ones, running competitive courses) want to meet applicants and find out whether they would cope with the demands of the course before making an offer.

Admissions tutors are seeking able students with academic potential in sufficient numbers to fill the places on their courses.

In deciding which applicants to accept, they are looking for the following.

- **Intellectual ability** – can you cope with the academic and professional demands of the subject and course?
- **Competition** – how well do you compare with other applicants for the course?
- **Applicants who are likely to accept** – if offered a place, is there a good chance that you will accept it?
- **Students who will make a contribution** – will you get involved in the life of the university or college and contribute in lectures, practicals and tutorials?
- **Applicants who are likely to get the grades** – are you expected to achieve the level of grades in your exams that this course generally requires?

And, very importantly!

- **Motivation**: a real and enthusiastic interest in the subject.

They may be able to find much of this information in your personal statement (see Chapter 23), but some will also use interviews to help them decide which applicants to make an offer to. There's usually no standard policy for each institution. In most cases admissions tutors themselves decide whom to interview.

In general, interviews are still used:

- for applicants with mitigating circumstances, or whose background would merit further consideration; also, mature students or those taking non-standard qualifications may be interviewed by some universities to assess their suitability for a course
- for borderline candidates – give it your best shot, because many admissions tutors like to give all applicants a chance
- for applicants who haven't studied the subject before – tutors need to know that you have researched it and know what's involved
- to distinguish between large numbers of similar, very able, applicants – particularly if you're applying for very competitive courses
- for vocational courses – those that lead to a particular career, e.g.:
  - agriculture
  - dentistry
  - health and social care
  - medicine
  - nursing
  - healthcare professions, e.g. physiotherapy, radiography, dietetics or occupational therapy
  - social work
  - teaching
  - veterinary science.

The majority of the above courses lead to work in a caring profession, which is why admissions tutors particularly need to be able to assess a student's suitability for the career. However, it's not unusual for applicants to courses in architecture or engineering to be interviewed, and they may also be asked to take examples of work or to talk about a project.

Universities and colleges that have a policy of calling applicants for interviews may arrange to conduct them by telephone, video-conferencing or Skype – usually for people who are unable to attend personally. This applies mainly to applicants who live outside the UK.

Your interview invite could come by letter or email or through your UCAS application. In all cases, you'll be offered a date and time. Instructions will be given on how to change these if they are inconvenient.

What will you be asked?

Interviews can take different forms. You could find yourself in front of just one person or an interview panel; or in a group, being observed as you discuss a topic or carry out a particular task. You may even be asked to take a written test.

Interview questions can be wide ranging and unpredictable – but, on the other hand, there are a few that tend to come up over and over again. Think about how you might respond to the following questions.

- Why do you want to study this subject?
- What aspects of your current studies have you found most interesting and why?
- Why have you applied to this department or faculty?
- Why have you chosen this university or college?
- What are your spare-time interests?
- Why should we offer you a place? (Don't be modest.)
- Tell me about an achievement you are proud of.
- What have you read outside your syllabus?
- What skills have you gained from your part-time job?
- Tell me more about the sports team/voluntary work/drama group you described on your application.
- Why are you taking a gap year and what are your plans? (If you're applying for deferred entry.)
- What have you learned about yourself from any work experience/ volunteering you have done?
- How have you coped with study in the Covid-19 pandemic? What has challenged you most, and how have you dealt with this?
- Have you any questions to ask? (This is a good way to demonstrate enthusiasm.)

You should also be prepared to talk about the following:

- your advanced-level study – what particularly interests you and what additional reading and research have you done?
- topical issues relating to your chosen subject
- anything you have mentioned in your personal statement.

For vocational courses, you can expect to discuss anything you've done to gain useful experience, such as work experience in a hospital, care setting, architectural practice, engineering company, accountant's or solicitor's office. Be prepared to describe what you did, what you learned and how the experience helped you to decide on your higher education course.

You may be asked about your understanding of the career you're thinking of, e.g. for medicine, what personal qualities do you believe a doctor should have? It's very important to keep up to date with developments in the career area you are exploring, especially if you're applying for subjects such as medicine or primary teaching. Websites such as www.gmc-uk.org (the General Medical Council) or www.tes.com (Times Education Supplement) are worth looking at, as interview questions are likely to ask about a particular issue relevant to that career.

Preparing yourself

Prepare as much as you can. Don't memorise or recite answers to any of the questions above – but think through the kind of things you would like to say. Taking the question 'Why should we give you a place?' as an example, you could:

- talk about your strengths, interests and ambitions, particularly with reference to courses you are interested in
- mention anything a bit individual or a little different that you can bring to share with others: for example, you may have debating experience, great rugby skills, extensive experience in charity fundraising or orienteering expertise; or you may have developed mentoring skills through your work as a sixth-form or college ambassador to 11–16-year-olds.

Ask your school or college to give you a mock interview – preferably with a member of staff who does not know you. This can be an excellent way of preparing yourself to think on your feet and answer unexpected questions, and you should get some helpful feedback.

Start thinking about interviews as early as possible. As you consider your course choices and compile a shortlist of universities and colleges to apply to, you should research answers to the questions admissions tutors might ask. If the admissions tutor asks 'Why have you chosen this university or college?', you'll then remember their particularly strong facilities or the unique angle of the course.

Try to keep interviews in mind as you write your personal statement (see Chapter 23). It is very likely that interviewers will use this as a basis for their questions, so don't mention anything you can't talk about and expand on. And, if you have a particular passion or area of interest in your chosen subject that you'd love to talk about, make sure you mention it in your statement.

Top tips for interviews

- Dress should be 'smart casual'. There's no need for it to be very formal. The interviewer probably won't be dressed formally either. As a general rule avoid jeans, and go for a skirt or smart trousers with a shirt, rather than a t-shirt. This holds true for virtual interviews using digital platforms too.
- Make eye contact with the interviewer. If there's more than one interviewer always reply to the person who asked the question – but look at the other/s from time to time to include them in your answer.
- Do your best to show you're thoughtful, committed and genuinely interested in your chosen subject.
- Always have one or two prepared questions of your own about the course, opportunities after you graduate or a relevant academic topic. (Don't ask questions only on topics covered in the material already published and sent to you by the university or college.)
- Make sure that you know exactly what you wrote in your personal statement.

- Don't bluff. If you don't know the answer to a question, ask the interviewer to repeat it or put it in a different way. If you still don't know, admit it!
- Most important – be sure you know exactly how to get to the interview. Check your travel arrangements. Make sure you're going to the correct site if the university or college has more than one. Allow plenty of time for your transport to be late and to find the right building and room when you get there.
- Take the interviewer's name and phone number with you so that you can call and explain if you're unavoidably delayed.

There are further useful tips on preparing for interviews and on what to expect on the UCAS website, www.ucas.com/invitations.

More detailed advice on interview technique and possible interview questions is given in the *Getting into* series (see the 'Resources' section below).

Auditions and portfolios

Your subject teachers will be able to offer more specific advice, but here are a few general points. If you're applying for a performance-based course in drama, music, dance or musical theatre, you will have to attend an audition – usually before an interview. (Some applicants are weeded out at the audition stage.) Policies vary at different institutions, but drama applicants can expect to be asked to:

- perform one or more pieces, often one from Shakespeare and one by a modern playwright – at some institutions, though, you are free to choose your own pieces
- deliver a monologue
- do some improvisation
- do some movement work
- work in a group.

You'll be sent detailed instructions on what to prepare for your audition.

Music students can expect to have to:

- perform at least two (contrasting) pieces – often from a set list – sent to you in advance – but sometimes of your own choice
- sight read
- improvise
- do technical tests (scales and arpeggios).

Dance students can expect to have to:

- participate in one or more dance classes, observed by teaching staff
- improvise

- perform a short piece choreographed by themselves
- participate in a group interview
- have an interview with one or more people which focuses on their future ambitions.

Sometimes a physical examination is included.

Music, drama, dance and musical theatre applicants can benefit from performing for a small audience before attending an audition. Your teachers may organise this automatically and arrange for you to perform in front of them and other students. You should then receive some feedback and constructive criticism.

Auditions are usually held in two parts. A group of students attend a first audition, then some are selected to attend a second or recall one. This often happens on the same day so that students successful in the first audition don't have the expense of returning on another date.

Art students normally have to take a portfolio of work with them – and will be expected to talk about it. You might be asked questions by one or two individual interviewers or you might be expected to display your pieces like a mini exhibition and explain how you developed and changed a piece as you worked on it. The usual advice is to:

- include some work that you have done on your own, i.e. not as part of coursework
- include notebooks and sketches as well as finished work
- bring photographs of three-dimensional work that is too heavy to take with you.

You'll be told what size your portfolio should be and how many pieces of work it should contain. However, some admissions tutors prefer to see portfolios in advance and assess them at the same time as they read the UCAS application. If so, you'll receive a request (usually by email) for your portfolio. The email you receive will tell you how to submit your portfolio – and full instructions will be given if you're expected to do so online.

It's a good idea to ask your art teacher to give you a mock interview and ask you questions on your portfolio.

Applicants for film-making and screen courses are expected to submit a different type of portfolio. You may normally include still work – photographs and art work – but the major element will be a short film lasting just a few minutes. (Timing is very important. Films that overrun aren't accepted.) You will be told whether you should use a set theme or one of your own, how many actors the film should include and whether to use an indoor or outdoor location. You'll be invited to explain your film and what you were aiming to achieve to the interview panel.

Aptitude tests

Many students now get top A level (or equivalent) grades, so admissions tutors for oversubscribed courses have no way of distinguishing between them. As such, several admissions tests have been devised to provide additional information that is relevant to their subjects. The most common tests are for medicine and law, usually the BMAT, the UCAT and the LNAT.

The BioMedical Admissions Test (BMAT): used by eight UK and overseas universities for admission to dentistry, medicine, veterinary science and biomedical sciences

This is a two-hour pen-and-paper test consisting of three papers.

1. **Thinking skills** – such as problem solving, understanding arguments, data analysis, critical thinking, logic and reasoning (60 minutes; 32 multiple-choice or short-answer questions).
2. **Scientific knowledge and application** – 27 questions requiring short or multiple-choice answers. This is designed to test knowledge typically included in non-specialist school science and mathematics courses and your ability to apply this knowledge. 30 minutes.
3. **Writing task** – a short essay from a choice of three titles. No prior knowledge is required. You'll be expected to develop ideas and explain them effectively. 30 minutes.

In 2020 the BMAT was taken on just one date (4 November), but from 2021 it has gone back to being available to sit on three dates each year: in February, September and November.

You may sit the BMAT at your school or college if it is a registered assessment centre, or at an 'open centre', which is a place that accepts external candidates.

As of December 2021, the fees for the BMAT are:

- £61 standard fee within the UK and the EU
- £92 standard fee outside the EU
- £34 additional late fee
- £36 application for results enquiries
- £36 application for appeal.

Check www.admissionstesting.org (the Cambridge Assessment Admissions Testing website) for up-to-date costs; here you can also access past questions and advice on how to prepare. If you're going to sit the test outside the UK, you should enquire whether the test centre you'll attend uses QWERTY, AZERTY or other keyboards.

BMAT® Thinking Skills Practice Questions

Have a go at the below sample BMAT Thinking Skills practice questions, taken from the full set.

DIRECTIONS (for full test):

Answer every question. Points are awarded for correct answers only. There are no penalties for incorrect answers. All questions are worth 1 mark.

3. The media frequently shares stories about the supposed dangers of screen time for children and teenagers, but there has been little discussion of the appropriate amount of screen time for adults. Recent research indicates that adults average 11 hours of screen time per day, which means that adults spend most of our waking time looking at screens. That figure has increased from nine and a half hours four years ago. Of the current figures, 43% of daily screen time is spent watching TV, 21% using smartphones, and 7% using tablets. This data underlines the fact that concerns about people spending too much time looking at smartphones are misguided, since adults actually spend significantly more time watching TV.

Which of the following is the best statement of the conclusion in the argument above?

A No one can say how much daily screen time is suitable for adults.

B It is unwarranted to worry that someone's smartphone screen time is excessive.

C Compared to smartphone usage, watching TV takes up more of the average adult's day.

D Adults spend more and more time looking at screens each year.

E There is not enough awareness of the dangers of screen time for adults.

4. The clocks in Beematia use an unusual format to indicate the time. Beematia uses a 24-hour clock in the format mm:hh, in which mm indicates the number of minutes to the next hour (hh). For example, 12:05 indicates the time is 12 minutes before 5am. Each day in Beematia has 24 hours and each hour has 60 minutes.

Srinand is visiting Beematia, and the clocks in his hotel room indicate the time in this format.

The clock in the hotel room says 19:22 when Srinand goes to sleep. When he wakes up, the clock reads 22:07.

For how long has Srinand slept?

A 2 hours, 45 minutes

B 7 hours, 41 minutes

C 8 hours, 57 minutes

D 9 hours, 3 minutes

E 10 hours, 19 minutes

UCAT (University Clinical Aptitude Test): used by UK and overseas universities for entry to medicine and dentistry

UCAT is an online test consisting of the following sections.

- **Verbal Reasoning:** designed to assess ability to think logically about written information and to arrive at a reasoned conclusion. 21 minutes.
- **Decision Making:** assesses ability to deal with various forms of information, to infer relationships, to make informed judgements, and to decide on an appropriate response to situations given. 31 minutes.
- **Quantitative Reasoning:** assesses ability to solve numerical problems. 24 minutes.
- **Abstract Reasoning:** assesses ability to infer relationships from information by convergent and divergent thinking. 13 minutes.
- **Situational Judgement:** measures capacity to understand real-world situations and to identify critical factors and appropriate behaviour in dealing with them. 26 minutes.

All answers are multiple-choice.

The test must be taken online at an approved test centre. There are centres in many countries around the world, as well as numerous centres within the UK, so you should be able to find one within convenient travelling distance.

At the time of writing, UCAT registration opens on 20 June 2022 for those wanting to start courses in 2023. These dates could be subject to change. As of March 2022, the fee for taking the UCAT in the UK is £70, and for taking it outside the UK it is £115.

If you plan to sit the test outside the UK, you should enquire whether the test centre you will attend uses QWERTY, AZERTY or other keyboards.

If you have any disabilities or additional needs that require you to have extra time in exams, make sure you register for the UCATSEN rather than the regular test. If you need special access arrangements for examinations, contact Pearson VUE customer services directly to discuss your personal requirements before booking the test.

Full information, including a guide to what to expect at a test centre, is given at www.ucat.ac.uk.

Law National Aptitude Test (LNAT): used by nine UK universities for entry to law

LNAT is a two-part online test that takes two and a quarter hours. It's designed to test the skills required to study law, but doesn't require any previous knowledge.

Section A consists of 42 multiple-choice questions based on argumentative passages. Candidates are given 95 minutes to answer all of the questions. For Section B, candidates have 40 minutes to answer one of five essay questions on a range of subjects and demonstrate their ability to argue economically to a conclusion, displaying a good command of written English.

You must take the LNAT assessment in whichever academic year you are applying to university (e.g. if you intend to start university in September 2023, you need to take it before January 2023). You can only sit the test once in the year, and results cannot be carried over from one year to the next. Registration for LNAT tests opens every August, with testing beginning in September.

Tests are offered at 500 centres around the world, including 150 in the UK. As of March 2022, the fee for taking the LNAT is £75 in the UK and £120 elsewhere. If you are going to sit the LNAT test outside the UK you should enquire whether test centres use QWERTY, AZERTY or other keyboards.

There is much more information on the LNAT website, www.lnat.ac.uk, where you can find out more about the different parts of the test and read some tips on both tackling multiple-choice questions and writing the kind of essay that will impress.

Can you prepare for BMAT, UCAT and LNAT?

You can't learn or revise anything for these tests. However, you can certainly prepare for them by finding out what to expect and practising, using practice papers, which are freely available online. You should also familiarise yourself with the type of equipment in the case of computer-based tests.

> **TIP!**
>
> Bursaries are available for applicants who would have difficulty in meeting the cost. Read full details on the test websites.

Other entrance tests

If you apply to either Oxford or Cambridge, you'll find that for many courses you'll be required to take an additional test. Cambridge has introduced common-format written assessments for all subjects except mathematics and music. You can very quickly find a list on the two universities' individual websites.

Many other universities and colleges also use entry tests for particular courses. You can find a full list of those that have been declared to UCAS, with details of how and where you can take them, on the UCAS website. The majority of tests are set and administered by the Admissions Testing Service, which is also responsible for BMAT. The two most common tests are the Sixth Term Examination Paper (STEP) and the Thinking Skills Assessment (TSA).

STEP (Sixth Term Examination Paper)

The test consists of up to three, three-hour, paper-based examinations. Candidates are usually required to sit either one or two of the examinations, depending on the requirements of the universities they have applied to. It is taken at the end of the second year of your sixth form or college study; it is normally sat at your school or college, or otherwise at a test centre. Currently, STEP is either required or recommended by the following universities: Cambridge, Warwick, Bath, UCL, King's College London, Southampton, Imperial, Bristol, Lancaster and Durham. Completion of STEP can lead to a lowered conditional offer. Mathematics departments in other universities may ask you to take specific STEP papers; you can check by looking on their websites.

If your school or college does not pay the fee, it is £93 per single paper taken in the UK, and £129 per paper taken outside the UK.

Thinking Skills Assessment (TSA)

This test is designed to test the sort of skills that are not always covered in school-based exams – such as critical thinking and problem solving. It is a pen-and-paper test consisting of two sections:

1. Multiple-choice questions: 50 questions covering problem solving (numerical and spatial reasoning) and critical thinking (understanding argument and reasoning using everyday language). Usually in multiple-choice format. 90 minutes.

2. Writing Task (not always used): tests ability to organise ideas in a clear and concise manner, and communicate them effectively in writing in a 30-minute essay chosen from four titles (on general topics – not linked to specific subjects).

The test is normally taken on the same day as an interview.

Currently the TSA is used by the universities of Oxford, Cambridge and University College, London for some of their courses. The test is free to take, but some test centres may charge a fee to use their service.

Mathematics Admissions Test (MAT)

Some universities prefer to use this pencil-and-paper test produced by the Admissions Testing Service in partnership with the University of Oxford. Current users are Oxford, Imperial College London and Warwick. The test takes 2 hours and 30 minutes. The University of Warwick does not insist on the test, but a good score may result in a reduced offer. The test is free to take, but some test centres may charge a fee to use their service. The MAT is taken in the fourth term of sixth form or college study.

Test of Mathematics for University Admission

This test is produced by the Admissions Testing Service.

Currently applicants are *encouraged* to take this test by the universities of Bath, Cambridge, Cardiff, Durham, Lancaster, LSE, Nottingham, Sheffield, Southampton and Warwick, which all state that a good score in the test may result in a lower advanced-level offer.

The test is normally taken in schools or colleges, but external test centres are available. As of December 2021, the fee is £57 for UK and EU students, and £75 for all others.

Test of Mathematics for University Admission Practice Question

1. $f(x)$ is a quadratic function in x.

The graph of $y = f(x)$ passes through the point $(1, -1)$ and has a turning point at $(-1, 3)$.

Find an expression for $f(x)$.

A $-x^2 - 2x + 2$

B $-x^2 + 2x + 3$

C $x^2 - 2x$

D $x^2 + 2x - 4$

E $2x^2 + 4x + 1$

F $-2x^2 - 4x + 5$

From Paper 1, 30 October 2019, permission kindly granted by Cambridge Assessment Admissions Testing.

Resources

Publications

- *Getting into* series, Trotman Education, www.trotman.co.uk. The series gives advice on securing a place at university for courses leading to professional careers (e.g. business and economics; dentistry; law; medicine; psychology; veterinary science); and on gaining a place on courses at Oxford and Cambridge.
- *Heap 2023: University Degree Course Offers*, Trotman Education, www.trotman.co.uk. Includes typical interview questions that arise for particular university courses; also, why students may be rejected.
- *University Interviews*, Trotman Education, www.trotman.co.uk.

Websites

- www.admissionstesting.org (BMAT, MAT, STEP and TSA).
- www.lnat.ac.uk (LNAT).
- www.maths.ox.ac.uk (MAT).
- ucas.com/trackyourapplication.
- www.ucat.ac.uk (UCAT).

NB: All the test websites offer free practice tests.

10 | Exam results and afterwards

This chapter looks at what might happen when you have your exam results. However, please don't skip the chapter and think 'I don't need to read this yet!' You might not need any of the information, but then again you might – and panic stations can set in in the summer. A lot of people whose exam results aren't what they hoped for make rushed decisions, leaping at the first option that presents itself. They can live to regret doing so.

This chapter discusses what happens at exam results time and the options you might have if you need or decide to change your plans. These include:

● Clearing
● rethinking your higher education plans, perhaps retaking certain subjects or taking different ones
● deciding not to do a higher education course at all.

Before results day

Most applicants are accepted conditionally before their exam results are known, so the results of exams taken or assessments completed in May/June are very important.

After you have taken your exams, you deserve to relax; but it is worth giving some thought to what you'll do if you don't get the grades needed for your higher education place – a sort of 'Plan B'. Will you try to secure a place through Clearing (see page 102)? Would you rather retake and apply again next year for the course you really want to do? Or are you having any doubts about whether higher education is really for you?

If you're ill or have some other problem at exam time that you think may adversely affect your results, tell the universities and colleges whose offers you're holding, or ask your school or college to contact them on your behalf. You may need to get a doctor's certificate to support your case. Admissions tutors will do their best to take such circumstances into account, but they'll need to know about them before your results come out. If you leave it until after you have disappointing results, it may be too late.

Results day

You will not see your results in your UCAS application. Your school, college or exam board will give your results to you.

Clearing vacancies will be available on www.ucas.com from 5 July.

IB results day for 2023 is yet to be confirmed at the time of writing, but is usually on the first Monday of July. Unless you plan to go to your school or college in person you will need to access them online via the 'candidate results website' a day later. You'll need the PIN and personal code that your IB programme coordinator will have given you earlier in the year. Remember to find out what time your results are released, as this is done at different times in different time zones; usually the UK receives them around 12 noon.

SQA results will be released in early August 2023. Your results will be sent to you to arrive in the post on results day. If you've signed up to MySQA and activated your account you can request to have these sent via email or text.

A level results are published in mid-August. You should be able to check your UCAS application from the morning onwards to see whether your place has been confirmed. But you won't see your results. You'll have to contact your school or college for them – usually by going in at a time you've been given. If admissions tutors are still considering whether to give you a place then your UCAS application won't be updated yet. Remember, that if you meet or exceed the exact terms of your offer your place is guaranteed. It's only people who have not done so who may need to wait.

UCAS receives most results from the exam boards. After checking they match the information on your application, UCAS sends them to the universities and colleges where you're holding any offers of a place. You can check at ucas.com/sending-exam-results to see the full list of qualifications UCAS do this for.

If your exams aren't listed, you'll have to send your results to your universities or colleges yourself. If you've taken any other exams, such as Nationals 4 and 5, GCSE or international qualifications, you must send your results as soon as you receive them to those universities and colleges where you are holding offers. (IB results may or may not be received by UCAS as schools and colleges need to give permission for this.)

When your results are released and have been received by the admissions tutors, they'll compare your results with the conditions they set and make a decision on whether to accept you.

If you get the grades

Congratulations! Your place will be confirmed – a university or college can't reject you if you have met the conditions of your offer by 6 September 2023.

> **TIP!**
>
> Arrange your holidays so you're at home when the results are published. Even if all goes well and your grades are acceptable, you may need to confirm your place and deal with your registration, accommodation and loan. And, if things haven't gone according to plan, you may need to take advice, find out about course vacancies and make some quick decisions about possible offers in the Clearing system (see below).

> **TIP!**
>
> You can check university and college decisions on results day.

If you missed out …

Don't panic! You should contact admissions offices immediately to find out whether they'll accept you anyway. Admissions tutors may decide to confirm your offer even if you failed to meet some of the conditions. It has been known for applicants to be accepted with much lower grades if there are places available, there's good school or college support and, perhaps, a good interview record – although this varies greatly from course to course. (But don't count on this!) Alternatively, you may be offered a place on a different course, but you don't have to accept this if you don't want to.

UCAS will send you an official notification of the outcome of your application. If you have been offered a place on an alternative course, you'll have a choice of actions. These will be listed in the notification letter.

If your place isn't confirmed, you can find a place through Clearing or Clearing Plus (see below); alternatively, you can retake your exams and apply again the following year.

Clearing

If you don't get the grades you had hoped for and your offer isn't confirmed, don't worry. If you're flexible and have reasonable exam results, there's still a good chance you could find another course through Clearing. In 2021, 56,225 students found places using this service.

You're eligible for Clearing if you paid the full application fee, you haven't withdrawn from the UCAS system and:

- you're not holding any offers (either because you didn't receive any, or because you declined the offers you did receive), or
- your offers haven't been confirmed because you haven't met the conditions (such as not achieving the required grades), or
- you made your UCAS application too late for it to be considered in the normal way (after 30 June).

Clearing Plus

Available alongside Clearing, Clearing Plus is a tool designed to help you find your perfect course.

To speed things up, UCAS takes what they know about you and what they know about the types of students universities and colleges are looking for, to suggest some courses you might like. You can express interest in courses, and the university or college can contact you.

Holding an offer, but changed your mind?

From 5 July, if you're holding a confirmed place and decide you no longer want it, you can use self-release into Clearing, by using the 'decline your place' button in your UCAS application. You should only use this button if you no longer want to take up your place at your firm choice, and you've spoken to your university or college and/or an adviser at your school/centre.

What do I have to do?

You need to find a course you're interested in that has vacancies. In your UCAS application, you'll be able to click through to a list of suggested course matches based on your qualifications and the courses you applied for previously. Here, you can follow the on-screen advice to connect with universities and colleges you're interested in.

Official course vacancies are also published in the UCAS search tool from early July until October. Arrangements for the publication of vacancies vary from year to year and precise sources of guidance for the summer of 2023 will be announced by UCAS closer to the time.

The national Exam Results Helpline on 0808 100 8000, which is staffed by trained advisers, is also a useful source of information and advice. You'll also see many advertisements for universities and colleges with vacant places in the national press.

Make a list of the courses you're interested in, and contact the institutions, in order of your preference, to ask whether they'll accept you. It's recommended that you telephone, email or visit in person

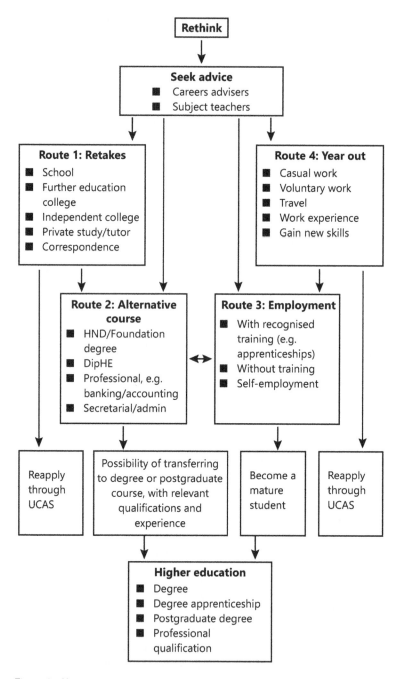

Figure 2: Alternatives to going to university in 2023

because the admissions tutor will want to speak to you personally, not to your parent or teacher. Keep your Clearing number (given in your UCAS application) to hand as you'll probably be asked for it. If you're not convinced that a course is right for you, remember you don't have to commit yourself. You just need to contact universities or colleges direct about any vacancies you're interested in.

If one agrees to give you a place on the course you want, you enter the institution and course details in your UCAS application and they'll then be able to accept you. Only accept an offer of a place when you're certain you have found the right course for you. Once you've accepted, you won't be able to take any further part in Clearing and you'll be committed to taking up your place. Figure 2 on page 107 gives tips on what you might do if you don't get a place through Clearing.

Top tips on Clearing

- Talk to your careers adviser about which courses and subjects would be most suitable for you, particularly if your original UCAS application was unsuccessful.
- Remember that you can apply for any course that has places left – you don't need to keep to the same subjects you first applied for. If you do decide to apply for courses that are quite different from the ones you originally selected, make sure you do your research thoroughly, referring back to prospectuses and websites. Remember, though, you won't be able to change your personal statement.
- Although you'll have to act quickly, don't make any hasty decisions – only accept an offer if you're sure the course is right for you.
- One way of making sure you're happy with your choice of course is to visit the university or college. Most universities and colleges are happy to make arrangements to meet applicants and show them around, and many will have Clearing open days. They know that you could be spending the next three or four years there, and will be reassured that you want to be sure you're making the right choice.
- If you're applying for art and design courses, you may need to supply a portfolio of work as well as your Clearing number.
- Remember that universities and colleges are likely to refer back to your UCAS application when deciding whether to make you an offer. So, it's a good idea to have another look at what you wrote on your personal statement to make sure you're familiar with it, just in case an admissions tutor wants to ask you about it.

When you've secured a place through Clearing

Make sure you get from your new choice of university or college the information you'll need about:

- accommodation
- term dates
- introductory arrangements.

Retakes

Remember, disappointing results don't have to mean the end of your ambitions. If low grades mean that you haven't been accepted on a course of your choice, you could consider retaking your exams, or you could change to a new subject if you think that would give you a better chance of improving your grades.

- Retakes of A levels and Scottish Highers are available only once each year – usually in June.
- IB retakes are available in both November and May. There are some restrictions, so you'll need to contact the centre where you might want to do your retakes.

While most university and college departments consider retake candidates – and some welcome the greater maturity and commitment to hard work that retaking demonstrates – be aware that you may be asked for higher grades. It's always worth checking with the relevant admissions tutor that your proposed retake programme is acceptable. It's very rare for Oxford or Cambridge to accept applicants who have retaken their exams, for example.

Part III
Your UCAS application

11 | Getting started

You can register at ucas.com and complete your application online. It's easy to use, accessible from any online device and:

- speeds up the processing of applying to higher education courses
- incorporates checks that prevent you from making simple errors
- is supported by the very latest UCAS course data and relevant additional information.

This chapter provides a brief outline of the application process. The following chapters explain each section of your online application.

Register for a UCAS account

The first thing you have to do is register.

- Click 'Sign in' on ucas.com.
- Click 'Register'.

Once you've registered you'll be asked a few questions about:

- when you want to start studying
- what level of study you're interested in, e.g. undergraduate if you're still at school or college; plus additional information on apprentice-ships and conservatoires if you'd like
- where you live – so UCAS can direct you to the right information
- your preferences – the information you can receive by email
- what you're interested in – three initial subjects you'd like to know more about.

> **TIP!**
>
> If you forget your password, you can use the 'Forgot your pass-word?' service on the login page.

Starting your application

When you log in to your account, you'll be able to mark as 'favourite' the courses you're interested in and view them in your hub anytime.

From 17 May 2022, you'll see the 'Your applications' tile in your hub. You can then start your application to study in 2023.

Applying via a school or college

Each year, all schools, colleges and careers centres registered with UCAS set up a unique password or 'buzzword', made up of at least six letters and numerals. This is used by you and all other UCAS applicants at your centre so that your application can be identified with that centre.

When you start your application you'll be asked if you're applying from a school, college or centre.

- Select 'Yes'.
- Enter the buzzword.
- Confirm the details are correct.

This links your application to your school, college or centre so they can support your application and add your reference.

You'll complete all the sections of your application – although you won't be able to see the reference on your application homepage, as this gets added by your school or college separately. The referee is likely to be one of your teachers, personal tutor or head of sixth form.

> **TIP!**
>
> The buzzword allows you to start your application, and lets UCAS see which centre you're from. Some centres are also set up as a **group**, which you can select for your type of application – your centre should let you know if that's the case.

Applying as an individual

If you want to apply, but you aren't attached to a school or college, you can easily make an application through ucas.com.

When you start your application you'll be asked if you're applying through a school, college or centre – just select 'No'.

From here, the only difference between making an application as an individual and making it via a school or college is how you provide a reference. You could ask your old school to supply your reference if you've left recently; you'll need to supply their buzzword in your application. When they've added the reference, they'll return your application to you to forward to UCAS.

You can enter an independent referee's details in the Reference section of your application; they'll receive an email from UCAS asking them to provide a reference directly onto your application through a secure website.

Your reference must be written by a responsible person who knows you well enough to comment on your suitability for the courses you've applied to. This could be an employer, a senior colleague in employment or voluntary work, a trainer, a careers adviser or the teacher of a relevant further education course you have recently attended. Your referee can't be a member of your family, a friend, partner or ex-partner.

> **TIP!**
>
> Make sure that you allow plenty of time for the person writing your reference to complete it before the UCAS application deadline. They may receive several requests at the same time. If you're a student at a school or college you'll probably be given an internal deadline.

Your written reference

The good news is, you're not allowed to write your own reference, so there's relatively little for you to do here. Your referee (usually a teacher if you're applying via a school or college) will write it and then attach it to your application, through their UCAS coordinator or administrator.

Having said this, it's important not to disregard your reference entirely. In some ways it's the most important item in the selection process. It's only your referee who can tell the admissions tutors about your attitude and motivation, and who can comment on your ability – so that admissions tutors aren't reliant solely on exam results and predicted grades.

Admissions tutors will be interested in:

- academic achievement and potential
- suitability and motivation for the chosen course
- predicted grades / personal qualities / career aspirations
- mitigating circumstances (such as illness or bereavement) that may have adversely affected a student's performance in previous examinations.

Referees are asked to estimate your level of performance in forthcoming exams, and these predictions of likely grades are important to your chances of acceptance. The best advice in this respect is to work hard and impress your referee!

Under the 2018 General Data Protection Regulations, you have the right to see your reference. Contact UCAS if you want to see all the information UCAS holds about you, including what your referee has written about you. There's now no such thing as a confidential reference.

Your reference will normally come from your current school or college, or the school or college you attended most recently. If you choose anyone else, make sure it's someone who can provide the kind of assessment higher education institutions need. Be aware, if you're attending a school or college, it will look very odd if you choose someone from outside as your referee.

If you have any difficulties at any stage, there's help within your application and on the UCAS website, or you can contact UCAS on 0371 4680 468 between 08:30 and 18:00 hours (UK time) on weekdays.

Navigating your application

From your application you can select English or Welsh, and choose to receive correspondence in your preferred language. You can change your preference back at any point.

The help text in your application is available in Welsh too. It is not possible to apply in any language other than English or Welsh.

Your application homepage

Your Personal ID will be displayed on the screen – make a note of this as you'll need it in future communications with UCAS and with universities and colleges.

Your homepage is where you'll see the sections that need to be completed. You don't need to complete the application all at once – you can log in and out at any time until you're finished.

As you add information to each tile, the 'Percentage complete' dial should increase each time you mark a section as complete.

See Figure 3, Welcome screen, page 112.

These are the different sections of your application:

- personal details
- contact and residency details
- employment
- education
- nationality details
- supporting information
- English language skills

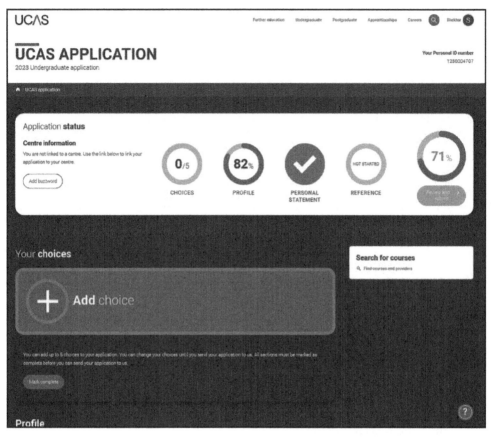

Figure 3: Welcome screen

- finance and funding
- diversity and inclusion (UK students only)
- more about you
- extra activities (UK students only)
- your personal statement
- choices.

You can access each section by clicking on its tile. There are on-screen instructions in every section, guiding you through what you have to do. If you get stuck at any point, you can access help text by clicking on the question mark in each section.

You're free to move between sections as you like, leaving them partially completed and returning to them later. When you've completed a section, just tick 'Mark this section as complete'.

Checking the progress of your application

As well as percentages of completion at the top of your application, each section will turn green when completed – with the confirmation 'Section complete'.

The tiles will give you an overview of whether a section is complete, in progress or needs to be started.

All sections must be marked as complete to send to UCAS. You must complete all mandatory questions – identified with an asterisk * – to mark a section as complete.

> **TIP!**
>
> Remember to save all your changes.

Once you've finished your application (and it's showing 100%), there are four steps to the submission process:

1. check your application – double check the details and download a PDF copy
2. update your preferences – e.g. what information about universities and student life you'd like to receive
3. confirm you've read and understood the terms and conditions
4. pay and submit – if you're applying through a school, college or centre they'll complete this (you'll just need to submit).

Once you've submitted your application to UCAS and received your welcome email, you can log in to your application to keep up to date with your progress and reply to your offers.

Security tips

To apply through ucas.com, it's recommended that you use the latest version of your chosen browser – as older versions may be less secure.

For data protection reasons, your application is in a secure area of the UCAS website. More recent web browsers have a built-in feature allowing you to save your password so that you don't have to remember or retype it later. However, if you use this facility it will allow anyone using that particular computer to log in to your account and change the details of your application. For this reason, it's strongly advised that you don't use this feature.

When you've finished a session in your application, it's strongly recommended that you log out properly by using the 'Log out' button (not by simply closing the window you are in). Once you've logged out, you should close your web browser down completely.

How the rest of this book works

The remaining chapters of this book will take you step-by-step through each section of your application, giving you general advice on the nature of the information you are asked for and the basic principles of getting it right.

Chapter 23 deals with finishing off your application, including information on:

- your declaration – your agreement with UCAS and higher education institutions
- submitting your application
- fee payment
- your reference.

At the end of the book you'll find a chapter on troubleshooting (Chapter 24), which will help you solve some of the most frequently encountered problems. Further help is available through the 'question mark' link on each section of your application.

Stop and think!

Before you start your application, here are some final tips and reminders.

- Make sure you've done all your research thoroughly and you're happy with your choices. If in doubt, take another look at Part I of this book, 'In the think tank'.
- Collect together:
    o your personal details
    o all school or college attendance dates
    o exam results slips and entry forms
    o any employment details (a copy of your CV is useful to have at hand)
    o details of the higher education courses you want to apply for, including institution and course codes (you can find these in the search tool on the UCAS website).
- Carefully read through the guidance available within your application.
- Be honest and truthful – you must be able to back up all your statements.

- Don't try to make more than one application in the same year.
- Remember, once your application reaches UCAS, you can't amend it or add anything to it. So, get someone – preferably someone who is well informed about higher education, such as a tutor – to check your personal statement.

You should now be ready to start your application – read on, and good luck!

12| Personal details

Obviously, UCAS and the universities and colleges you're applying to need to know who you are and how they can contact you. They'll also need to know about a number of other aspects of your life. This can be for important financial reasons (e.g. in deciding who assesses your eligibility for funding), or to check whether you need any additional support while studying, for example if you have a disability.

Your application will, therefore, contain quite a lot of information about you, which we'll go through step by step in the upcoming chapters.

Personal information

The name you entered when you registered will have been drawn through into the personal details section of your application. You'll also be asked to provide your:

- title
- previous name(s) – including by marriage or deed poll
- preferred name – what you would like to be called, e.g. Matthew or Matt
- date of birth – required for UCAS' and institutions' records.

> **TIP!**
>
> Don't provide nicknames. It is important that you enter the same names that appear on official documents such as exam certificates.

The list on the left of each section will show which sections are completed (with a tick), which are in progress (with a half moon), and which haven't been started yet (no icon).

If you'd like more information about a section, click on the question mark link for help text to provide advice about what to put.

13 | Contact and residency details

In this section you'll be asked to provide:

- a contact phone number
- your postal address
- whether you want to nominate anyone else to act or speak on your behalf about your application
- whether your home address is the same as your postal address – if not, you can provide a separate home address
- your residential details – choose the option that most closely applies to you.

Postal/home address

You can provide both a postal and a home address if you want to.

Your postal address is the one where written correspondence about your application will be sent. This doesn't have to be your home address.

If you decide to give your school address, you'll need to provide your home address as well.

Nominee access

You'll have the option of naming one person who can act on your behalf regarding your application. It's a good idea to do so, in case of illness or injury, for example. You just need to fill in their name and their relationship to you.

Residential category

Residential category can be complicated, but it's particularly important because what you enter here will be the point from which universities and colleges will start to classify you as 'home' or 'overseas' for the purpose of tuition fees. Those classified as overseas students pay a much higher annual tuition fee. (Your tuition fee status has no direct connection with your nationality – it depends on your place of ordinary residence and the length of time you have been ordinarily resident there.) You must choose from a list of residential category options (as defined by UCAS), summarised below.

UK citizen – England, Northern Ireland, Scotland, Wales, Channel Islands and Isle of Man, and British Overseas Territories

You're a UK citizen, or are the child or grandchild, or the spouse or civil partner of a UK citizen and have lived in England, Northern Ireland, Scotland, Wales, the Channel Islands and Isle of Man, or British Overseas Territories for the past three years, but not just for full-time education. If you've been living in any of these regions for three years partly for full-time education, you also lived in any of these regions prior to that three-year period.

EU national

You're an EU national, or are the child or grandchild, or the spouse or civil partner of an EU national, and have lived in the European Economic Area (EEA) or Switzerland or European Overseas Territories (OT) for the past three years, but not just for full-time education. If you've been living in the EEA or Switzerland or OT for three years partly for full-time education, you also lived in the EEA or Switzerland or OT prior to that three-year period.

EEA or Swiss national

Either: You're an EEA or Swiss national working in the UK, or you're the child, spouse or civil partner of such a person or you're the parent or grandparent of an EEA national working in the UK. You've lived in the EEA or Switzerland or OT for the past three years, but not just for full-time education. If you've been living in the EEA, Switzerland or OT for three years partly for full-time education, you also lived in the EEA, Switzerland or OT prior to that three-year period.

Or: You're the child of a Swiss national and have lived in the EEA or Switzerland or OT for the past three years, but not just for full-time education. If you've been living in the EEA, Switzerland or OT for three years partly for full-time education, you also lived in the EEA, Switzerland or OT prior to that three-year period.

Child of a Turkish worker

You're the child of a Turkish national who has lawfully worked in the UK, and you've lived in the EEA, Switzerland or Turkey for the past three years.

Refugee

You've been recognised as a refugee by the British government or you're the spouse, civil partner or child under 18 of such a person at the time of the asylum application.

Humanitarian Protection or similar

You've been granted Exceptional Leave to Enter or Remain, Humanitarian Protection or Discretionary Leave or you're the spouse, civil partner or child under 18 of such a person at the time of the asylum application.

Settled in the UK

You have Indefinite Leave to Enter or Remain in the UK or the Right of Abode in the UK and have lived in the UK, the Channel Islands or the Isle of Man (or more than one of these) for three years, but not just for full-time education. (However, this does not apply if you're exempt from immigration control, for example, as a diplomat, a member of visiting armed forces or an employee of an international organisation or the family or staff member of such a person; if this is your situation your residential category is Other.)

Other

If you don't fit any of the above categories then answer 'Other'.

Universities and colleges will try to be fair to you, but they do have a duty to apply the regulations equitably to all their students. Before applying, you could write to universities and colleges outlining your circumstances. Some overseas companies have standard letters for employees to use. It sometimes happens that different universities and colleges will classify the same student in different ways, depending on their reading of the rules.

TIP!

If you cannot find your area on the list, you need to look through the existing options to find one that matches your circumstances.

14| Employment

It's very useful for admissions tutors to know if you've had a job, particularly if you've worked in an area relevant to your application or chosen career. Include paid full-time and part-time roles – even weekend jobs – but only if you worked in them for a reasonable period. Even if the jobs were just to earn pocket money, an admissions tutor will see this as a broadening of your experience. (Note that institutions won't contact previous employers for a reference without your permission.)

> 'Work experience, whether paid or unpaid is useful to write about on a personal statement. If, for example, someone is applying for nursing, if they have done jobs in areas such as retail they will have gained some useful experience. Jobs such as these involve working in teams and helping customers, both of which require people-handling skills that are necessary for nursing. Also, being a nurse involves being in a position of considerable trust, and so anything that applicants have done that requires them to be honest and trustworthy is also very good to write about on the personal statement, e.g. handling money or being responsible for others in some way. I like to see what the applicant is like as a whole person, as having the right personal qualities is essential for a career in healthcare.'
>
> *Admissions tutor for Nursing*

Add your employment

- Click 'Add employment'.
- Fill in the employer's name (i.e. the company/organisation name) and address, your role title, start and end dates, and whether it is/ was full or part time. If the job you are entering is where you are employed currently, you don't need to enter a finish date.
- If you add more than one instance of employment experience, they'll appear in chronological order, with the most recent at the top.
- Remember to mark the section as complete, even if you haven't created an employment record.

See Figure 4, Employment, opposite.

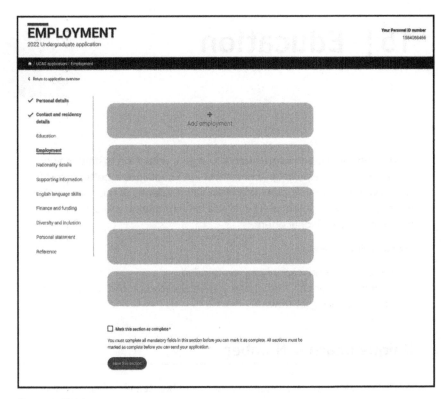

Figure 4: Employment

15 | Education

It's essential to include information about your education to date in your application. This helps to give universities and colleges a better idea of who you are, as well as providing them with evidence of your academic achievements and potential. They'll use the information you give here to put together conditional offers.

This chapter covers:

- the places of education you've attended
- your qualifications – both those you've already completed and those you're studying for now.

Unique Learner Number

You'll be asked for a Unique Learner Number (ULN). You probably won't have one of these – if so, just leave the question blank. Though you may have a ULN if you started studying for a UK qualification from 2008 onwards. If so, enter it in the box provided – it should be ten digits long (i.e. only numbers).

Places of education

You need to add details of where you've studied, or are studying – including any schools or colleges overseas.

- Start by clicking 'Add place of education'.
- Type the name of where you studied. Once you find your centre, click on the name and the Exam centre number will automatically populate if the centre has one (many don't, so don't worry if this remains blank).
- Add when you started and finished, and if you're still studying there add the month you're due to finish.

See Figure 5, Add places of education, opposite.

Enter all the secondary schools, colleges and universities you've attended (up to a maximum of ten). If you've attended more than this,

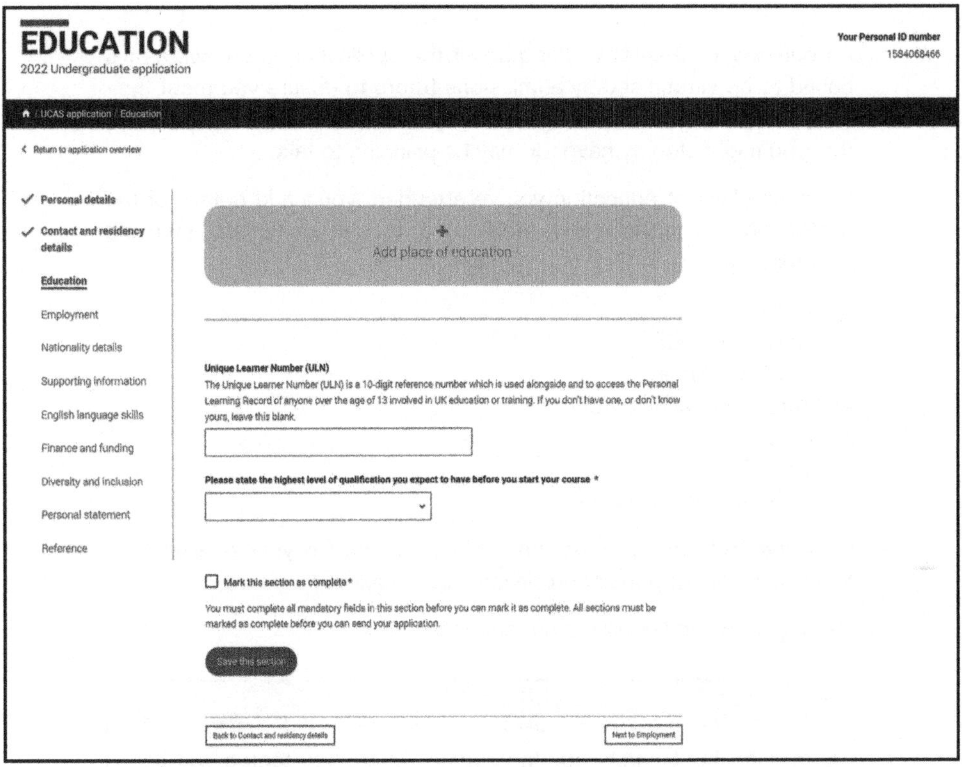

Figure 5: Add places of education

enter the ten most recent. If you've spent any time at a higher education institution you need to say so – and be prepared for questions about it if you're invited to an interview.

If, after typing the school name, a result does not appear, you can add this manually by clicking 'add' underneath. You can then type the name of the school into the box, or type 'home-school' if your secondary education has all been home-based.

TIP!

There are warning messages to help you – e.g. you can't say you attended two or more places of study full-time during the same date range. Red text means something is wrong and blue text is information you need to be aware of.

Add qualifications

As outlined in Chapter 6, this part of the application is crucial, as it's bound to be scrutinised by admissions tutors to ensure you meet their entry requirements. There are so many different kinds of qualification that you might already have, or may be planning to take.

For each place of education you've attended, you'll add details of the qualifications you achieved there, and those you're still studying towards, e.g.:

- A level
- Advanced VCE
- BTEC Diploma
- European Baccalaureate
- GCSE
- T level
- Irish Leaving Certificate.

Click the 'Add qualification' button and search for your qualification. You'll see a list of popular qualifications, or search for yours.

See Figure 6, Add qualification, opposite.

> **TIP!**
>
> Enter into the 'Search' box the country where you took a qualification, and you will find a list all the qualifications for that country.

Enter the details for each qualification

The qualification dates you can select are based on those you entered when you added your place of education.

If you know which awarding organisation it is, enter it here – speak to your teacher or tutor if you're not sure.

If you haven't finished the qualification or had your result yet, then select 'Pending'.

See Figure 7, Add qualification details, page 126.

You'll also be asked to enter information about the modules or units you've taken, and the unit grades you've achieved in qualifications that have been completed and certificated (e.g. GCE AS exams). Entering unit details is optional, but could be worth doing if you had some exceptional results or completed a highly relevant module to the courses you're applying to.

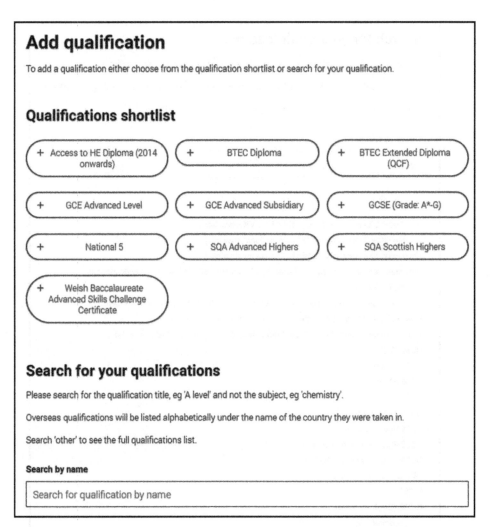

Add qualification

To add a qualification either choose from the qualification shortlist or search for your qualification.

Qualifications shortlist

+ Access to HE Diploma (2014 onwards)

+ BTEC Diploma

+ BTEC Extended Diploma (QCF)

+ GCE Advanced Level

+ GCE Advanced Subsidiary

+ GCSE (Grade: A*-G)

+ National 5

+ SQA Advanced Highers

+ SQA Scottish Highers

+ Welsh Baccalaureate Advanced Skills Challenge Certificate

Search for your qualifications

Please search for the qualification title, eg 'A level' and not the subject, eg 'chemistry'.

Overseas qualifications will be listed alphabetically under the name of the country they were taken in.

Search 'other' to see the full qualifications list.

Search by name

Search for qualification by name

Figure 6: Add qualification

If you entered a Scottish qualification, you'll be prompted to enter your Scottish Candidate Number. If you don't know your number, ask your college or check your exam certificate.

Some BTEC qualifications will also ask for your BTEC Registration Number – ask your school or college if you're not sure what this is.

Putting the right information on your UCAS application is important. Incorrect or incomplete information can cause problems for your university or college and could result in inaccurate or delayed decisions.

Once you've entered all the qualifications you've completed or are yet to complete, click 'Save this section'.

Search for your qualifications

Please search for the qualification title, eg 'A level' and not the subject, eg 'chemistry'.

Overseas qualifications will be listed alphabetically under the name of the country they were taken in.

Search 'other' to see the full qualifications list.

Search by name

gcse

AQA Level 1/Level 2 Certificate (iGCSE for UK State Schools)
Applied GCSEs (formerly GCSEs in Vocational subjects)
Applied GCSEs (formerly GCSEs in vocational subjects)
Bahamas General Certificate of Secondary Education (BGCSE)-West Indies/Caribbean
Cambridge IGCSE
Cambridge International Level 1/Level 2 Certificate (iGCSE for UK State Schools)
Edexcel Level 1/Level 2 Certificate (iGCSE for UK State Schools)
Edexcel Level 1/Level 2 Certificate Double Award (iGCSE for UK State Schools)
GCSE (9-1)
GCSE (Applied)
GCSE (Grade: 9-1)
GCSE (Vocational)
GCSE Combined Course
GCSE Short Course
GCSE: Double Award (9-9 to 1-1)
GCSE: Double Award (A*-A* to G-G)
HIGCSE (International)
IGCSE
IGCSE (Double Award)
International GCSE
International GCSE (9-1)
International GCSE (Double Award) (9-9 to 1-1)
International GCSE (Double Award) (AA to GG)
Level 1 /Level 2 Certificates (Ofqual-approved IGCSE, e.g. for UK state schools)
Level 1/Level 2 Certificates Double Award (iGCSE for UK State Schools)
Oxford AQA Exams International GCSE
Oxford AQA International GCSE
WJEC Level 1/Level 2 Certificate (iGCSE for UK State Schools)
West Indies/Caribbean-Bahamas General Certificate of Secondary Education (BGCSE)
iGCSE

Figure 7: Add qualification details

> **TIP!**
>
> You can return to the education area of your application, to edit or add to the entries already made, up to the point when you submit your application through your UCAS coordinator.

Which qualifications should I add?

Qualifications you've already received

You should list all qualifications for which you've received certification from the awarding body (this will usually include GCSEs, Scottish Nationals 4 and 5, and other GCSE-equivalent qualifications). Include all the qualifications you've taken, even if you didn't pass them. You mustn't conceal anything because you'll have to declare at a later stage that you've entered complete and accurate information.

You may be asked to supply original certificates to support the qualifications listed in your application at any time during the application process. You must include details of these qualifications even if you're planning to retake, whether completely or only in part. (You can explain your reasons for retaking in your personal statement.)

If you're a mature student with no formal qualifications, enter 'No formal qualifications'. (See page 158 for advice on how you can address this issue in your personal statement.) If you're hoping to enter university or college via APL or APEL, you should contact your chosen institution before applying to UCAS. Mature students should complete this section as fully as possible – many forget to list their present college.

If you're an international student, you need to give full details of all your qualifications in the original language. Do not try to provide a UK equivalent. If your first language is not English but your qualifications were completely or partly assessed in English, make this clear. You should also provide details of any English language tests you have taken or plan to take, giving dates, titles and any syllabus codes.

Send a copy of all transcripts, certificates or other proof of your qualifications direct to each university or college you apply to, quoting the title and code number of the course and your UCAS Personal ID once you have submitted your application to UCAS. Do not, however, send anything of this sort to UCAS.

> **TIP!**
>
> If you feel there are genuine reasons why some of your grades were lower than expected, make sure the person who's going to write your reference is aware if this and can explain the reason.

Qualifications you're currently studying for

You must also enter details of all qualifications that you're studying for now and those for which you're awaiting results. These may include A levels, Scottish Highers and Advanced Highers, BTEC qualifications, NVQs, Access courses and so on.

> **TIP!**
>
> If you have one, take your full Progress File (a record of your personal development, skills development and achievements) with you if invited for interview. You could even send a brief summary direct to the institution, quoting your Personal ID. You can then discuss and explain what your file comprises, and how it was developed.

16 | Nationality details

UK nationals

You're asked to confirm your country of birth and nationality – this information is for statistical purposes only, to find out where applicants come from. It won't be used for selection purposes.

If you were born in the UK, you should select 'United Kingdom' for your country of birth and 'UK national' for your nationality – i.e. you can't select 'Scotland', 'English'.

See Figure 8, UK nationality questions, below.

NATIONALITY DETAILS
2022 Undergraduate application

Your Personal ID number
1584068466

UCAS application / Nationality details

Return to application overview

✓ Personal details

✓ Contact and residency details

ⓘ Education

Employment

Nationality details

Supporting information

English language skills

Finance and funding

Diversity and inclusion

Personal statement

Reference

What is your country of birth? *
For the purpose of this question the UK includes the Channel Islands and the Isle of Man.

United Kingdom

What is your nationality? *
If you're applying from outside the UK choose your nationality as it appears in your passport. If you have dual nationality and you need a visa to enter the UK, enter your first nationality as it is shown on the passport you intend to use when travelling to the UK for your course.

UK national

Dual nationality
If you have dual nationality, select your first nationality in the previous field and your second nationality here.

☑ Mark this section as complete *

You must complete all mandatory fields in this section before you can mark it as complete. All sections must be marked as complete before you can send your application.

Save this section

Back to Employment

Next to Supporting information

Figure 8: UK nationality questions

International

If you were born in the UK but have a different nationality, you'll be asked additional questions. The information you provide will help universities and colleges to determine your eligibility – and allow them to assist you with the visa application process if needed.

If you weren't born in the UK, you're asked for the date of first entry to the UK.

If you're not in the UK yet, put the first day of the month you plan to arrive.

Visa and passport details

If you select 'Yes' when asked if you will need a visa, you'll also be asked for your passport details. If you don't have a passport yet, you can provide these details to your university or college when you receive an offer.

See Figure 9, Nationality, visa and passport details, opposite.

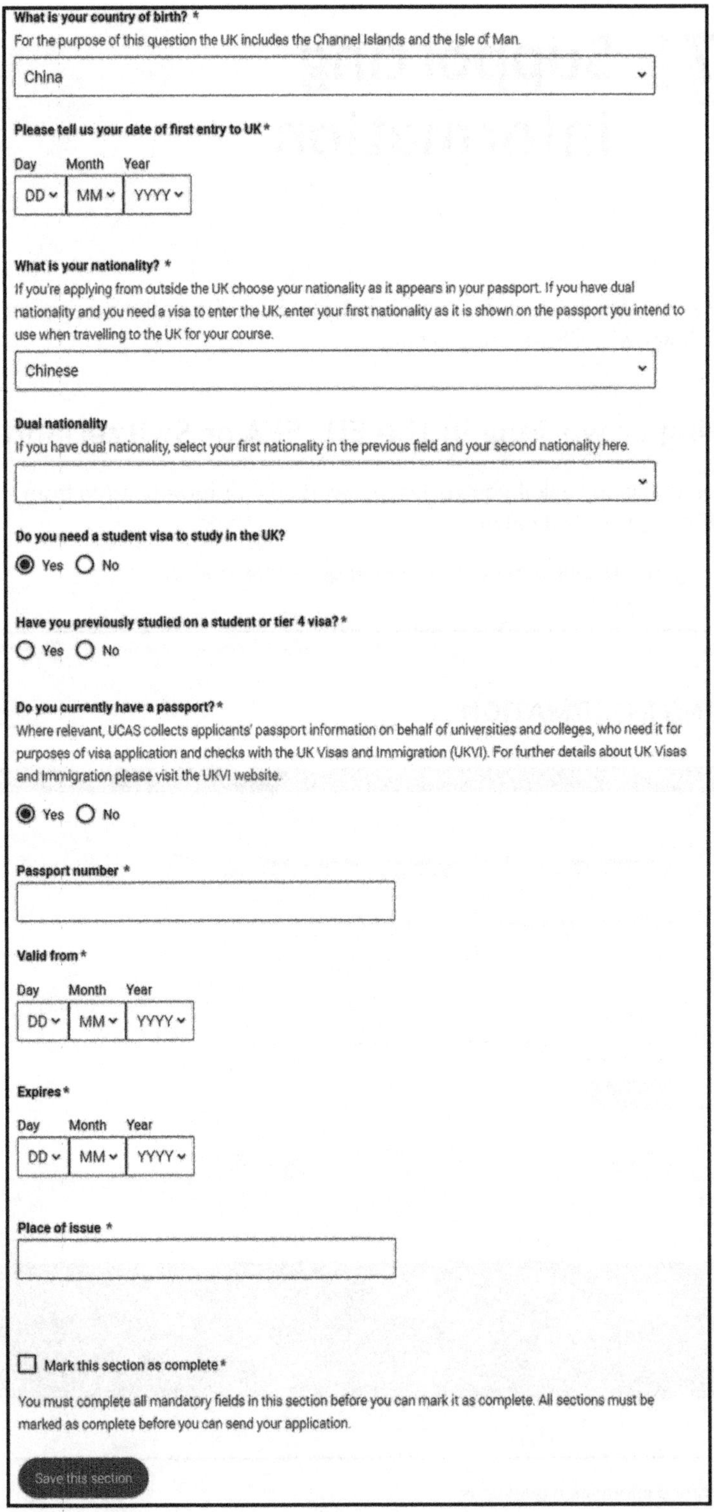

What is your country of birth? *

For the purpose of this question the UK includes the Channel Islands and the Isle of Man.

China	⌄

Please tell us your date of first entry to UK *

Day   Month   Year

DD ⌄	MM ⌄	YYYY ⌄

What is your nationality? *

If you're applying from outside the UK choose your nationality as it appears in your passport. If you have dual nationality and you need a visa to enter the UK, enter your first nationality as it is shown on the passport you intend to use when travelling to the UK for your course.

Chinese	⌄

Dual nationality

If you have dual nationality, select your first nationality in the previous field and your second nationality here.

	⌄

Do you need a student visa to study in the UK?

◉ Yes   ○ No

Have you previously studied on a student or tier 4 visa? *

○ Yes   ○ No

Do you currently have a passport? *

Where relevant, UCAS collects applicants' passport information on behalf of universities and colleges, who need it for purposes of visa application and checks with the UK Visas and Immigration (UKVI). For further details about UK Visas and Immigration please visit the UKVI website.

◉ Yes   ○ No

Passport number *

Valid from *

Day   Month   Year

DD ⌄	MM ⌄	YYYY ⌄

Expires *

Day   Month   Year

DD ⌄	MM ⌄	YYYY ⌄

Place of issue *

☐ Mark this section as complete *

You must complete all mandatory fields in this section before you can mark it as complete. All sections must be marked as complete before you can send your application.

(Save this section)

Figure 9: Nationality, visa and passport details

17 | Supporting information

These questions are mandatory(*), but you have the option to answer 'I don't know' or 'Prefer not to say'.

Living or working in the EU, EEA or Switzerland

These questions ask if you've lived or worked – or have parents from – the EU, EEA or Switzerland.

See Figure 10: Supporting information questions, below.

Figure 10: Supporting information questions

18 | English language skills

If English isn't your first or primary language, this section asks for your Test of English as a Foreign Language (TOEFL) or International English Language Testing System (IELTS) registration numbers.

If you've registered for, or already hold, either of these English language tests (for international students), enter your registration number in the relevant field.

See Figure 11, English language skills, below.

Figure 11: English language skills

19 Finance and funding

You'll only be asked further questions on finance and funding if you select 'UK, ChI, IoM or EU Student Finance Services' (United Kingdom, Channel Islands, Isle of Man, European Union).

You'll also be asked you for your local authority under 'Student support arrangements'.

For more information on funding and other financial concerns see Chapter 3 or ucas.com/finance.

See Figure 12, Finance and funding, below.

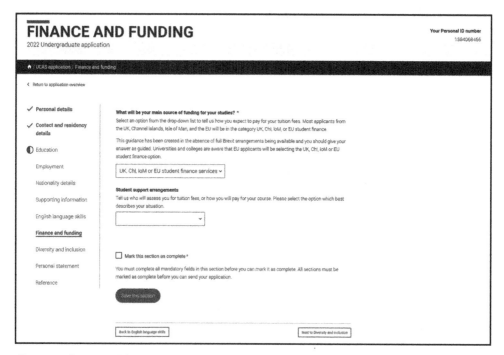

Figure 12: Finance and funding

Sponsorship

If you're applying for sponsorship you can give the name of your first-choice sponsor in the personal statement section of your application (see Chapter 23). You can find out more about company sponsorship from a careers adviser.

Also make a note in your personal statement if you plan to defer to 2024 if your application for sponsorship is unsuccessful this year.

20 | Diversity and inclusion

You'll only see this section if you have a UK home or postal address. It covers:

- equality monitoring:
  - ethnic origin
  - religion or belief
  - sexual orientation
  - identifying as transgender
  - national identity
- parental education
- whether you would like to receive correspondence in Welsh
- occupational background.

Don't worry about the equality monitoring

Universities and colleges have a legal obligation to make sure applicants are not discriminated against or disadvantaged. They only see this information after you've secured a place or at the end of the application cycle – so it doesn't influence any decision making. It's used to ensure applications are treated fairly.

There are two mandatory fields(*), but you have the option to respond with 'I prefer not to say'.

See Figure 13, Diversity and inclusion, opposite.

Ethnic origin

You're asked to select your ethnic origin, or the category that most closely describes it. The options are:

- white
- gypsy, traveller or Irish traveller
- black – Caribbean
- black – African
- black – other background
- Asian – Indian
- Asian – Pakistani

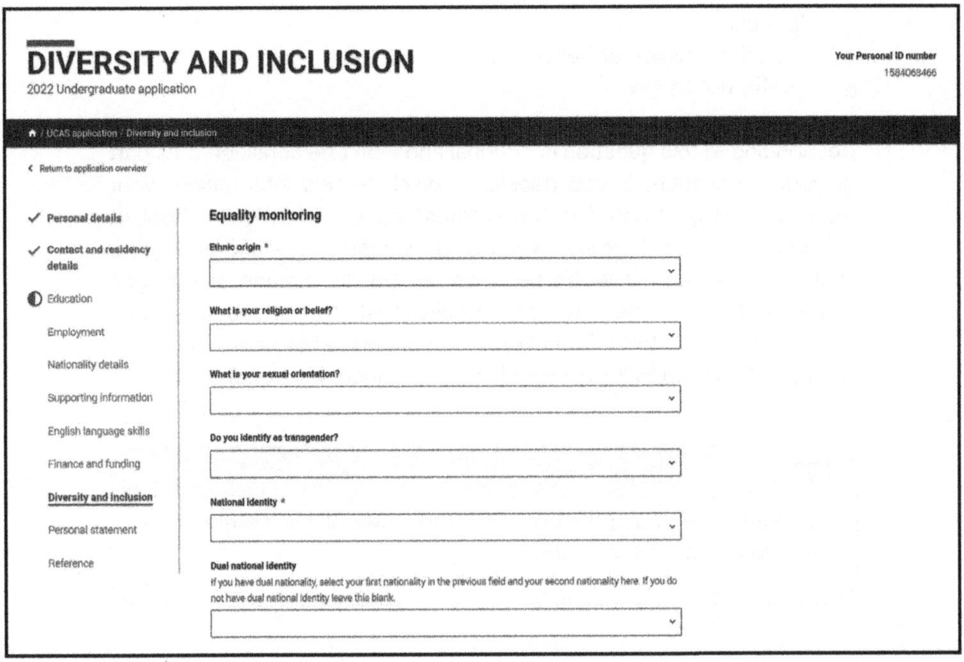
DIVERSITY AND INCLUSION
2022 Undergraduate application
Your Personal ID number
1584068466
/ UCAS application / Diversity and inclusion
< Return to application overview
✓ Personal details
✓ Contact and residency details
Education
Employment
Nationality details
Supporting information
English language skills
Finance and funding
Diversity and inclusion
Personal statement
Reference
Equality monitoring
Ethnic origin *
What is your religion or belief?
What is your sexual orientation?
Do you identify as transgender?
National identity *
Dual national identity
If you have dual nationality, select your first nationality in the previous field and your second nationality here. If you do not have dual national identity leave this blank.

Figure 13: Diversity and inclusion

- Asian – Bangladeshi
- Asian – Chinese
- Asian – other background
- mixed – white and black Caribbean
- mixed – white and black African
- mixed – white and Asian
- mixed – other background
- Arab
- other ethnic background
- I prefer not to say.

Religion or belief

You're asked to select your religion or belief from a drop-down list:

- No religion or belief
- Buddhist
- Christian
- Hindu
- Jewish
- Muslim
- Sikh

- Spiritual
- Any other religion or belief
- I prefer not to say.

Responding to this question is optional and won't be considered as part of your application. If you decide to disclose this information, your response will be treated in the strictest confidence. Your school or college, adviser and referee won't have access to it – and during the application process it won't be seen by the universities or colleges you're applying to. The university or college where you secure a place will have access to this information once your place has been confirmed. All data disclosed will be stored in compliance with data protection legislation.

> **TIP!**
>
> You must enter one of the options listed – even if it is 'I prefer not to say' – to complete the section.

Sexual orientation

You're asked to select your sexual orientation from a drop-down list:

- Bisexual
- Gay man
- Gay woman/lesbian
- Heterosexual
- Other
- I prefer not to say.

As with the 'Religion or belief' section, responding to this question is optional, and won't be considered as part of your application.

Transgender

You'll be asked if you identify as transgender, and to select from a drop-down list:

- Yes
- No
- I prefer not to say.

As with the 'Religion or belief' section, responding to this question is optional, and won't be considered as part of your application.

National identity

You'll be asked to classify your national identity. This is different from ethnicity and nationality and can be based on many things – for example culture, language or ancestry/family history.

You'll need to describe your national identity using the options listed below. You can use either one option – for example 'Welsh'. Or you can use two options if you feel you have dual national identity – for example 'English' and 'Scottish', or 'Irish' and 'Other' if you are Irish with a national identity not listed. If you feel you have more than two national identities, you should select 'Other' for one or both options.

- British
- English
- Irish
- Scottish
- Welsh
- Other
- I prefer not to say.

Parental education

You'll be asked whether or not either of your parents, or your step-parents or guardians, have any higher education qualifications – such as degrees, diplomas or certificates of higher education. If you're unsure, select 'Don't know' from the drop-down list. If you don't want to disclose this information, you can select 'I prefer not to say'.

See Figure 14, Parental education and occupational background, below.

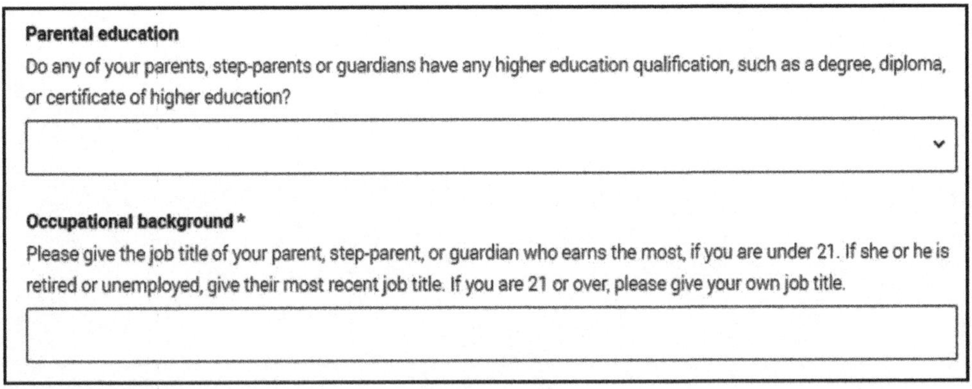

Parental education

Do any of your parents, step-parents or guardians have any higher education qualification, such as a degree, diploma, or certificate of higher education?

Occupational background *

Please give the job title of your parent, step-parent, or guardian who earns the most, if you are under 21. If she or he is retired or unemployed, give their most recent job title. If you are 21 or over, please give your own job title.

Figure 14: Parental education and occupational background

Occupational background

If you're aged under 21, you should give the occupation of your parent, step-parent or guardian who earns the most. If they're retired, give their most recent occupation. If you're 21 or over, you should give your own occupation. Enter at least three characters of the job title in the search box and select the job title you want. If you prefer not to give this information, please enter: 'I prefer not to say'.

This information is converted into occupational classifications based on those used by the Office for National Statistics, and is used to help monitor participation in higher education across all parts of society. NB: This information won't be released to your chosen universities or colleges until after a decision has been made regarding your application.

21| More about you

If you have a home or postal address outside the UK, you will only see the question asking if you have a physical and/or mental health condition, long-term illness, or learning difference. The other questions are for UK residents only

This section gives you the option to highlight your individual circumstances. Universities and colleges can make more informed decisions about your circumstances and make sure supportive measures are in place for you.

See Figure 15, More about you, page 143.

Students with a physical and/or mental health condition, long-term illness, or learning difference

Every year, over 60,000 students with a physical and/or mental health condition, long-term illness, or learning difference apply through UCAS to study at a university or college in the UK, and access a range of support available to help with their studies, day-to-day activities, travel, or lifestyle. The information you give in the application will help them do this.

Telling a course provider about a health condition or impairment early means they can work to make the arrangements or adjustments ready for your arrival. However, if you decide not to give this information now, you can do so after you have sent your application, by contacting them directly.

The information you provide here may also be used (anonymously) for monitoring purposes to inform and improve support for future students.

Select the option(s) you feel best describes any physical and/or mental health condition, long-term illness or learning difference you may live with. If you have no impairment or condition, select 'None'. If you want to give details of more than one option, you can do this in the further text box.

You'll be asked if you consider yourself as living with any of the following:

- a learning difference (e.g. dyslexia, dyspraxia, or AD(H)D)
- a visual impairment uncorrected by glasses (e.g. blindness or partial sight)
- a hearing impairment (e.g. deafness or partial hearing)

- a physical impairment or challenges with mobility (e.g. climbing stairs or uneven surfaces), or dexterity (e.g. using a keyboard or laboratory equipment)
- a mental health condition, challenge or disorder (e.g. anxiety or depression)
- a social, behavioural or communication impairment (e.g. an autistic spectrum condition or Tourette's Syndrome)
- a long-term illness or health condition which may involve pain or cause fatigue, loss of concentration or breathing difficulties – including any effects from taking associated medication
- a condition or impairment not listed above (you will be asked to give further details)
- two or more impairments or conditions (you will be asked to give further details)
- none.

Estranged students

An estranged person is someone who no longer has the support of their parents, and often also other family members, due to a permanent breakdown in their relationship which has led to ceased contact. This might mean your biological, step or adoptive parents or wider family members who have been responsible for supporting you in the past.

Select 'Yes' if you feel this description applies to you.

If you select 'Yes', your information will be treated in confidence, to help the university or college provide support for you. It may also be used for monitoring purposes to inform and improve support for future students who are estranged from their parents.

Students with caring responsibilities

Select 'Yes' if you're responsible for providing unpaid care to someone who has, for example:

- a long-term illness
- a disability
- a mental health condition
- an addiction
- temporary care needs following, e.g., an accident or operation.

If you select 'Yes', your information will be treated in confidence, to help the university or college provide the right support for you. It may also be used for monitoring purposes to inform and improve support for future students who have care responsibilities.

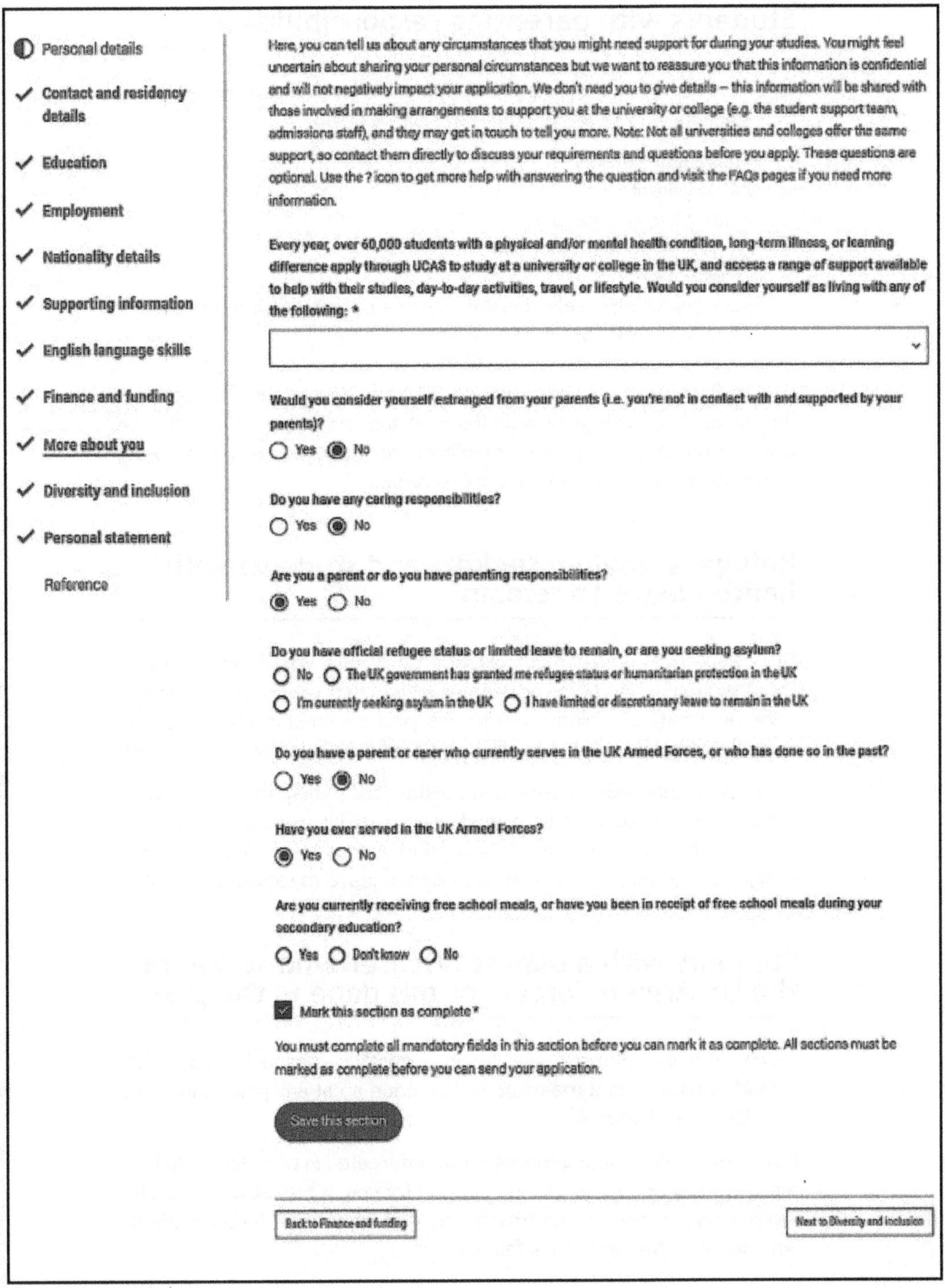

Personal details

Contact and residency details

Education

Employment

Nationality details

Supporting information

English language skills

Finance and funding

More about you

Diversity and inclusion

Personal statement

Reference

Here, you can tell us about any circumstances that you might need support for during your studies. You might feel uncertain about sharing your personal circumstances but we want to reassure you that this information is confidential and will not negatively impact your application. We don't need you to give details – this information will be shared with those involved in making arrangements to support you at the university or college (e.g. the student support team, admissions staff), and they may get in touch to tell you more. Note: Not all universities and colleges offer the same support, so contact them directly to discuss your requirements and questions before you apply. These questions are optional. Use the ? icon to get more help with answering the question and visit the FAQs pages if you need more information.

Every year, over 60,000 students with a physical and/or mental health condition, long-term illness, or learning difference apply through UCAS to study at a university or college in the UK, and access a range of support available to help with their studies, day-to-day activities, travel, or lifestyle. Would you consider yourself as living with any of the following: *

[⌄]

Would you consider yourself estranged from your parents (i.e. you're not in contact with and supported by your parents)?

○ Yes ◉ No

Do you have any caring responsibilities?

○ Yes ◉ No

Are you a parent or do you have parenting responsibilities?

◉ Yes ○ No

Do you have official refugee status or limited leave to remain, or are you seeking asylum?

○ No ○ The UK government has granted me refugee status or humanitarian protection in the UK

○ I'm currently seeking asylum in the UK   ○ I have limited or discretionary leave to remain in the UK

Do you have a parent or carer who currently serves in the UK Armed Forces, or who has done so in the past?

○ Yes ◉ No

Have you ever served in the UK Armed Forces?

◉ Yes ○ No

Are you currently receiving free school meals, or have you been in receipt of free school meals during your secondary education?

○ Yes ○ Don't know ○ No

☑ Mark this section as complete *

You must complete all mandatory fields in this section before you can mark it as complete. All sections must be marked as complete before you can send your application.

(Save this section)

[Back to Finance and funding]   [Next to Diversity and inclusion]

Figure 15: More about you

Students with parenting responsibilities

Select 'Yes' if you're a parent, or responsible for the care and wellbeing of a child aged 17 or under. This can include being:

- a biological parent
- a step-parent
- an adoptive or legal parent
- a legally appointed guardian
- a foster carer
- someone who provides kinship or other parental care to the child of a family member or friend.

If you select 'Yes', your information will be treated in confidence, to help the university or college provide the right support for you. It may also be used for monitoring purposes to inform and improve support for future students who have parenting responsibilities.

Refugees, asylum seekers and students with limited leave to remain

Select the option that most closely represents your circumstances. Don't worry if your choice doesn't exactly match your residency status – the university or college will discuss your circumstances with you in more detail to decide if you qualify as a 'home' or 'international' student.

Your information will be treated in confidence, to help the university or college provide support for you. It may also be used for monitoring purposes to inform and improve support for future students who are refugees or asylum seekers, or with limited leave to remain in the UK.

Students with a parent or carer who serves in the UK Armed Forces, or has done in the past

Select 'Yes' if you have a parent who currently serves in the regular UK Armed Forces or as a reservist, or has done so at any point during the first 25 years of your life.

If you select 'Yes', your information will be treated in confidence, to help the university or college provide support for you. It may also be used for monitoring purposes to inform and improve support for future students who are from Armed Forces families.

Students who have served in the UK Armed Forces

Select 'Yes' if you have served as a Regular or Reservist in the UK Armed Forces (including: the Royal Navy, Royal Marines, British Army, Royal Air Force, or Merchant Mariners who have seen duty on military operations).

If you select 'Yes', your information will be treated in confidence, to help the university or college provide support for you. It may also be used for monitoring purposes to inform and improve support for future students who have a Service background.

Students receiving free school meals

Young people in the UK are usually eligible for free school meals if their parents or carers are on a low income or in receipt of certain benefits. If you're not sure, ask your school – they will be able to confirm this for you.

You may also be eligible if you're paid qualifying benefits directly, instead of through your parent or carer.

22 | Extra activities

You'll only see this section if you have a UK home or postal address.

If you've participated in an activity to prepare you for higher education you can give details of it here. You can select the activity from a drop-down list. For example: national or regional schemes, university-run programmes, summer schools, campus days, taster courses and booster courses. You can also use your personal statement to include more details about the activities you took part in, the skills you learned, and how this prepared you for higher education.

NB: Open days are not relevant to this question.

If you haven't attended any such activity, please leave this section blank.

If this section is relevant to you, you'll be asked to give the following details:

- the type of activity [drop-down list]
- the activity provider [drop-down list]
- the name of the activity/programme [free text box – optional]
- the start and end date of the activity.

See Figure 16, Add activity, opposite.

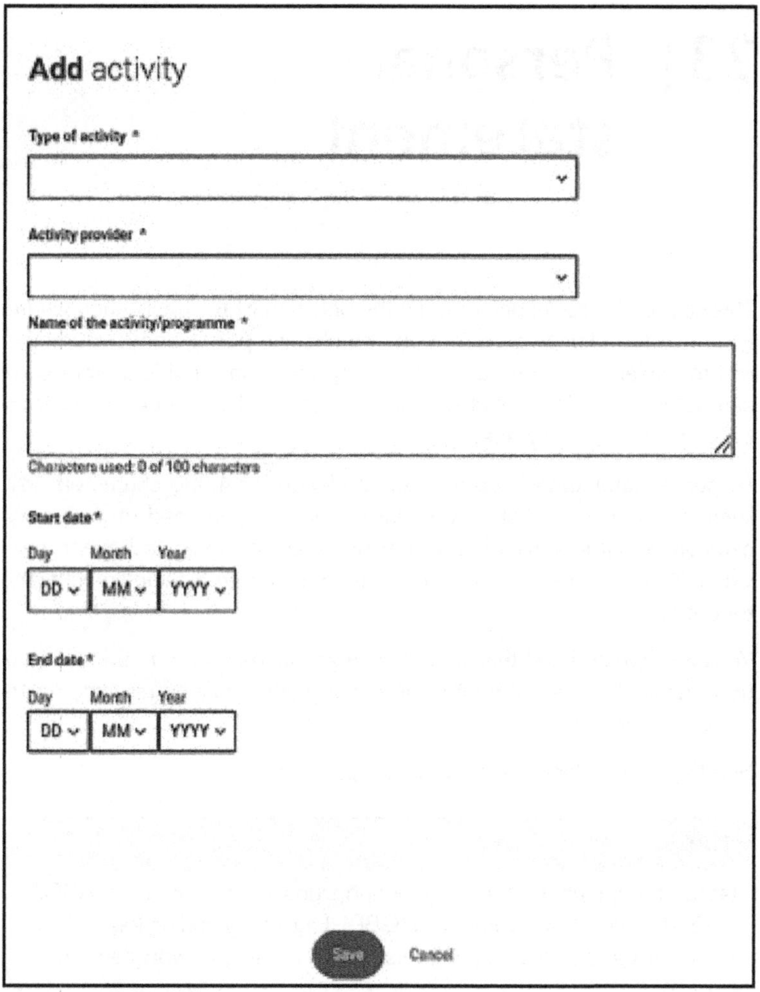

Add activity

Type of activity *

| ⌄ |

Activity provider *

| ⌄ |

Name of the activity/programme *

Characters used: 0 of 100 characters

Start date *

Day   Month   Year

| DD ⌄ | MM ⌄ | YYYY ⌄ |

End date *

Day   Month   Year

| DD ⌄ | MM ⌄ | YYYY ⌄ |

Save   Cancel

Figure 16: Add activity

23 | Personal statement

This section is crucial because it's the only part of the application where you have the chance to select and emphasise points about yourself – and to explain to admissions tutors why you're interested in your chosen subject(s). It's your chance to impress and convince admissions tutors to offer you a place.

Personal statements have a maximum length of 4,000 characters (47 lines) and a minimum of 1,000 characters – so you need to think very carefully about exactly what you want to say in the limited space provided. You can click on 'Save' at any time to update the line and character count.

You can save and edit this section as many times as you need to. If you try to navigate away without saving your work, you'll be reminded with a pop-up warning.

See Figure 17, Personal statement, opposite.

> **TIP!**
>
> Note: 'foreign characters' e.g. pound signs are converted to ASCII/Unicode – so '£' will convert to 'GBP'. University and college admissions tutors will be expecting this, so it's nothing to worry about.

What are admissions tutors looking for?

Factual information

The admissions tutors will want to know about:

- your career aspirations – many higher education courses aren't job-related, so don't worry if you don't have a clear idea of your future career direction, unless of course you're applying for a vocational course
- your reasons for choosing the course(s) – wherever possible these should be backed up by evidence of particular reading or additional things you've done that have reinforced your commitment to your chosen subject

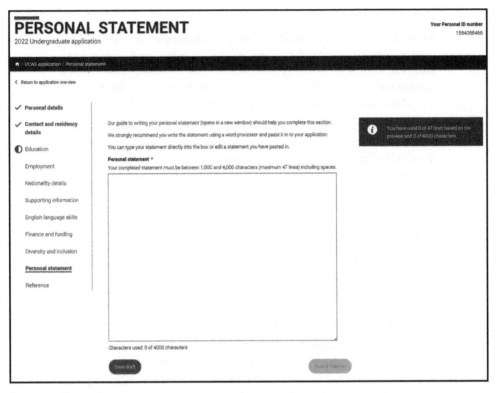

Figure 17: Personal statement

- relevant background or experience – which could include work experience/work shadowing, practical activity in music or theatre, attendance on courses, time abroad, etc. (evidence of practical experience may be vital to the success of an application to a medical or veterinary school, and may also significantly help your application if you're applying for some management and engineering courses)
- any interests you may have (e.g. Duke of Edinburgh's Award, charity fundraising, painting, potholing, positions of responsibility) – these may not seem strictly relevant to the course, but they help to give an impression of you as a person
- the name of any sponsor you may have – relatively few students are sponsored through their course and you will not be at a disadvantage if you have nothing to mention; but if you have applied for sponsorship, universities and colleges are keen to know whether you've been successful, or to where you've applied.

Reading between the lines

Your statement will convey more about you than just the bare facts. The way you present the facts will give valuable clues about other qualities such as critical thinking and communication skills.

Analytical skills

Admissions tutors are usually looking for students who can analyse their current experience. A common weakness is that applicants tend to describe what they're doing now, rather than analysing their current experiences and relating them to what they hope to get from higher education and their future career prospects.

Alongside the descriptive approach tends to be a listing of data already entered in the application (e.g. present studies) or details of apparently unrelated hobbies. Hobbies are an important part of your statement, but they need to be analysed in the context of how they have contributed to your skills or personal development in a way that would be an indicator of success on the courses you've applied for.

Communication skills

The text and presentation of your statement provide the admissions tutor with an indication of your communication skills – from grammar and spelling to your ability to express information and ideas clearly.

Maturity

A good statement provides evidence of maturity of thought and a sense of responsibility. If you intend to study away from home, it's important to show that you have these attributes, as they indicate that you'll be likely to adapt well to your new environment.

TIP!

It's difficult for an applicant who has selected a wide range of disparate courses to give feasible reasons for having done so, which is why this approach isn't recommended.

Top tips

Impression. Think about the impression you want to give – try to show you're interested and interesting, bright, mature and eager to learn.

Structure. Organise what you want to say into a logical structure and make sure that everything you say is clear and concise. Use subheadings if you think it will help.

Length. Do not try to pack too much in – it can get confusing. Deliver your main points well, rather than saying a little bit of everything.

Relevance. Explain why each point you mention is relevant. Do not unnecessarily repeat anything that appears elsewhere on your application.

Honesty. It's so important to be honest and specific. If necessary, be selective – claiming too much is not always a good idea.

Accuracy. Check your spelling. The UCAS application doesn't have a spell-check facility, so it's worth typing your statement in something like a Microsoft Word document so you can spell-check it first, then copy and paste it into the personal statement section of the application. Get someone else to read it through, too – it's sometimes hard to spot your own mistakes, and computer spell-checkers aren't infallible.

Placing 'leads'. Admissions tutors are likely to use your statement as inspiration for interview questions. So, only mention things you're prepared to talk about at an interview. If there's something you would particularly like to be asked to discuss, you can give the interviewer a lead by mentioning it in your statement.

And finally ...

Check up on yourself. Read critically through everything you've written. Try to imagine you're the admissions tutor, trying to pick holes in what you've said. You may also find it useful to work with friends and read through each other's drafts – you'll be surprised how often a friend will say to you, 'But haven't you forgotten ...?'

TIP!

You can find advice on completing your personal statement and a tool to help you think about what to include at: www.ucas.com/personalstatement and in the book *How to Create a Winning Personal Statement,* Trotman Education.

Advice on writing the personal statement

The personal statement is a very good opportunity for you to demonstrate your interest and motivation in the subject(s) you want to study.

- Be concise in your use of language – sentences should be kept short and to the point. Admissions tutors must read hundreds of personal statements and don't want to wade through clunky paragraphs, especially if they are not relevant.
- Avoid using vague, worn-out clichés, like 'I have good communication skills'. What does this mean to someone who doesn't know you? Better to say, 'In my role as a student mentor to younger pupils in school, I have developed my

listening skills and how to communicate information to them effectively. I have needed to consider their level of vocabulary and understanding.'
- If you don't know where to start, look at some examples of personal statements written by previous applicants (see below for examples).
- Never plagiarise (this means copying work of others claiming it to be your own work). Plagiarism is easy to spot these days as UCAS and universities have access to powerful computer tools to detect this.
- Wherever possible, give examples of things you've done, what you learned from the experiences, what you learned about yourself and how they're relevant to your application.
- As you write the personal statement, read it aloud to yourself – that way you can see if it flows well, or repeats words and phrases.
- Avoid spelling and grammatical errors! These look particularly bad if you're applying for an academic degree such as English Literature!
- Demonstrate interest and enthusiasm for the subject(s) you want to study at university. Give examples of additional reading you've done, activities you have taken part in, e.g. summer schools or taster events.
- Have a beginning, middle and end. The opening sentences set the direction of the personal statement, the middle gives the evidence of your motivation and suitability, and the end draws the parts together with a summary and conclusion.
- Get someone else to read it! A sixth form or college tutor are obvious examples – preferably someone who is knowledgeable and up to date with applying to higher education.

TIP!

Save your work regularly to keep the line count updated – and click to preview your statement.

Creating a winning personal statement

Amazingly, every year there are a few applicants who leave the statement section completely blank. Obviously this is inadvisable, to say the least! But many others do themselves no good simply as a result of the way they present information.

Good sample personal statements

Kyle - Economics (2,871 characters)

My case for wanting to study economics at university is based on several factors, which I would like to illustrate in this personal statement.

Subscribing to the *Economist* and reading texts such as *Starting Economics* by George Stanlake and *Brilliant Economics: Making Sense of the Big Ideas* by Phil Thornton has confirmed to me that economics is the subject I want to study at university. I am particularly interested in exploring how economics affects us all, from the poorest communities in developing countries to the richest in western capitalist nations, thanks to reading *Poor Economics* by Abhijit Banerjee & Esther Duflo and *Flash Boys* by Michael Lewis.

I have completed a nine-week long Massive Open Online Course (MOOC) by the University of Warwick called 'Big Data'. I found this fascinating, as it illustrated how researchers are currently studying the topic of Big Data, a field of study I could potentially be involved with in the future. The course also enabled me to develop basic programming skills in 'R Studio' for data analysis. I am registered to take part in another MOOC – 'Discovering Business in Society' – run by the University of Exeter, which will teach the basics of how businesses work and how they connect with the greater socio-economic environment.

I enjoy listening to economics articles on Radio 4 and take an interest in current affairs through reading newspapers such as the *Times*, the *Financial Times* and the *Guardian*. This helps me keep up to date with national and international economic issues, and I believe it has given me a good foundation of knowledge and understanding of economics and helped me achieve strong grades in essays set on my A level economics course.

The broad range of subjects I am studying at A level has helped me to develop a range of skills that are relevant to the study of economics at university. Problem solving in mathematics has given me the ability to approach problems in a logical and reasoned manner; I have also learnt to persevere and try different approaches to tackling mathematical problems. Chemistry has helped me to analyse the results of experiments and present them in a clear and structured manner; it has also given me the opportunity to practise forming conclusions based on data collected. History and economics have taught how me to analyse and formulate arguments, as well as write clearly and concisely to ultimately present a well-structured essay.

Outside of my formal studies, I work as a part-time customer service assistant in the retail sector. This has enhanced my time management skills (balancing my A level study commitments with a job), as well as my confidence in dealing with a wide range of people encountered in a busy retail environment. I believe this experience will help me make the transition from school to university more easily.

I am a member of the school council, and have represented the school in hockey tournaments. I play piano to grade 4 standard – the need to practise has taught me self-discipline and how perseverance helps one to develop and improve.

My subject motivation, self-discipline and curiosity for new knowledge, I believe, make me a strong candidate for studying economics at university. I look forward to the opportunity of studying this key subject to degree level after my A level studies.

Andrew - Mathematics (3,768 characters)

From an early age I was very good at solving puzzles; I soon learned that I was also strong in my ability to solve problems and work things out in a methodical and logical way. Naturally, mathematics quickly became a favourite subject for me throughout my primary and secondary education, leading to an A* grade in my GCSE. I wanted to study this subject in greater depth and so A level Mathematics and Further Mathematics were natural progressions for me.

A levels have been challenging, but also incredibly interesting. In my A level Further Mathematics, I have been fascinated by decision mathematics, including critical path analysis, which has been the most rewarding topic in my studies so far. I am curious to deepen and expand my knowledge in this field more widely. I have enjoyed all my mathematics modules, with pure mathematics being the most interesting as it focuses on thought processes and problem solving, in particular differentiation and integration.

Outside of lessons, I spend many hours each week practising methods learned; it is vital to get a good understanding of all topics, as mathematics is a continuous subject where earlier knowledge is needed to be able to fully grasp future ones.

A level Chemistry is strengthening my mathematical skills too owing to the large number of calculations required in topics such as chemical equations, calculating molarity and speed of atoms.

Studying chemistry demands that I grasp applied mathematical concepts, and the application of mathematics further helps me solve chemical problems.

I have discovered that mathematics can be used to describe and predict a wide range of things, including the speed of chemical reactions, the rate of acceleration of vehicles, planetary motion and the ways that decisions are reached in business. The skills I have developed and will go on to develop further at university will enable me to work in many industries where mental agility and reasoning are required.

In my first year of A level studies, I undertook work experience in a primary school where I was a classroom assistant helping children with their subjects, in particular mathematics. Throughout my work experience I gained confidence talking to others, undertook problem solving (e.g., supporting students experiencing difficulties with subjects), and communicated with teachers. My work experience has formed part of my Duke of Edinburgh Gold Award which I am due to complete in the next few weeks. Beyond studying mathematics at university, I am looking to train as a mathematics teacher where I can pass on the knowledge and skills I have gained to others. I love working with children and helping them to develop their learning; I found it incredibly rewarding to see that 'light bulb' moment when a child suddenly understood how to work out a number problem and the confidence this gave them to build their knowledge further.

Outside of my studies, I enjoy sport, including athletics; I am a county-level, middle-distance runner. I am competitive and disciplined in my training, and good physical health and fitness have enabled me to approach my A level studies with more energy and personal drive. I believe that my willingness to study hard outside of my lessons is a good preparation for university level study where even more independent learning is required than at A level. My sporting activities have required me to stay away from home on some occasions, and so I am accustomed to being away from my family and meeting new people.

I believe that a university education will not only greatly expand and deepen my knowledge of mathematics, but enable me to experience new challenges and meet new people from different backgrounds and cultures, thereby helping me to prepare for adult and working life more effectively.

Roderick - Nursing (3,295 characters)

If you were to have asked me five years ago what my career aspirations were, nursing would not have been on my list. However, 2019 was the ultimate turning point for me, when my beloved sister lost her battle to pancreatic cancer. Witnessing first-hand the care, nurture and support both my sister and family received through the district nurses, sparked a fire within me that I could not quench. This led me to further investigate what it really takes to become a nurse.

The primary role of a nurse is to advocate and care for individuals and support them through health and illness. However, there are various other responsibilities under the umbrella of healthcare. Nursing requires one to passionately care for all types of patients, provide emotional support, ensure a high standard of care, and utilise exceptional communication skills to provide a calming bed-side manner.

As every moment is experience, the past six months have been spent working at St Andrew's Healthcare as a healthcare assistant. This has given me a valuable insight into a working hospital environment, but also solidified my expectations of the professional standards of practice and behaviour that must be upheld, the importance of delivering efficient patient care while maintaining the patient's dignity, and patient confidentiality.

Being a nurse requires various skills. My past work experiences have contributed to my development, ranging from hospitality and events manager at Aston Villa Football Club where my leadership skills were honed, to volunteering in an outpatient physiotherapy department where I was able to successfully follow instructions and complete tasks given to me. Both experiences have taught me valuable lessons: the importance of communication, and the strength of teamwork while being able to effectively work independently within the scope of my competence.

I undertook the Science Foundation Year, which gave me an excellent academic grounding. I was able to develop my exam techniques, research skills, essay writing and language vocabulary. I have also studied a BTEC National Diploma in Applied Science. This course, which is essential in nursing, covers all the sciences and includes specific units such as Anatomy, Physiology of the Human Body Systems, Physiology of Human Regulation and Microbiological Techniques.

I have a great passion for sport, including athletics, badminton and basketball. I particularly enjoy traveling and experiencing new cultures. Alongside this, I have a keen interest in landscape photography. It is important to me to have a healthy balance of both physical and mental growth.

In line with the NMC code of practice, I am fully aware of my duty of care; this includes knowing my limitations. I am enthusiastic and confident within my scope of practice. I am a competent team player, always willing to seek the guiding hand of my senior colleagues. I take pride in my multifaceted career; I know that healthcare is not prescriptive, however I am able to transpose theory into practice. I have experience in being flexible in adapting to a changing work environment, and I can rise and meet the many challenges in the profession. I believe the attributes and skills I have gained, academically and in my work experience have given me an excellent foundation to pursue a career in nursing.

TIP!

If you want to supply more information than the statement space allows, once your application has been processed and you've received your welcome email, you can send information directly to your chosen universities or colleges, quoting your Personal ID. (Do not send it to UCAS.)

Subject-specific advice

The personal statement is especially important in subjects such as **creative and performing arts**. Say what you've done, seen or heard – do not be one of the music applicants who do not actually mention their chosen instrument!

Applicants for **teacher training, medicine, veterinary science, dentistry** or **physiotherapy** courses should be sure to give details of work experience (including locations and dates).

If you are currently studying for a **vocational or occupational qualification** that your admissions tutors may be unfamiliar with, explain the relevance of your studies to the course(s) you're applying for.

If you are an **international** student, explain why you want to study in the UK. Can you provide evidence that you will be able to complete a course run and taught in English?

If you're into **sport**, give details of your achievements, e.g. 'I play tennis for my county', showing you're committed to something you excel in.

It is wise to check with admissions staff at universities about how they feel about students taking gap years *before* you apply. Institutions will vary on this – some will be happy for you to take a year out, others may not be, and others may require (or at least prefer) you to do something during the year that will enhance your studies. Don't just assume they'll accept you taking a gap year. If you plan to take a gap year, it is advisable to cover your reasons for doing so in your personal statement. Remember that anything you say is likely to be used as a basis for questions if there's an interview. The two examples below show common pitfalls.

Example 1

'In my gap year I hope to work and travel.'

Comment

This statement is far too vague and would cause many admissions tutors to wonder whether you had really good reasons for deferring entry, or whether you were just postponing the decision to take up a place on their course.

Example 2

'In my gap year I hope to travel to gain work experience.'

Comment

This is likely to lead to questions such as: What kind of work experience? For how long? Is it relevant to your chosen course? How? Where? What will you do while you are there? Try to be as specific as possible. This candidate's statement would have been better if they had explained what sort of work experience they wanted and what drew them to their chosen country.

In contrast, the following gives a clear indication of a well-planned gap year.

Example 3

'For my gap year I have arranged a work experience placement in my local primary school. This will be for two days per week from September 2021 until July 2022 and will include helping children with reading, assisting class teachers in preparation of lessons and materials to be used in art and craft sessions, as well as accompanying staff and pupils on outside visits. This, I believe, will give me invaluable experience in the classroom which will support my intended degree in primary education. I will also be travelling to the USA for one month in the summer where I will stay with relatives for part of this time. This will give me experience of another society and culture as well as getting me accustomed to being away from home.'

Mature students

You must say what you've done since leaving school. If, like many mature applicants, you've had a variety of occupations and experience, you may find the UCAS application too restrictive. So, you could summarise your career on the application and then send a full CV direct to your chosen universities or colleges. However, there is enough space for you to present your background and interests in a fair amount of detail.

Everyone's circumstances are different, but the following example is the kind of thing that might attract favourable attention from an admissions tutor.

Example

- 1997–2002: Left school with GCSEs in four subjects at grade C, including mathematics and a grade B in English language.
- 2002–2005: Completed mechanical engineering apprenticeship.
- 2005–2018: Worked with two engineering companies until my redundancy.
- 2018–2021: While unemployed, I took a part-time pre-access course and also volunteered at a training centre for people with moderate learning difficulties and also befriending the elderly in a nursing home.
- September 2021–date: I have been studying on an Access to Higher Education Diploma in social sciences.

I had grown tired of working in engineering and took the opportunity to change career direction towards one where I could help and support people. My aim is to qualify as a professional social worker by taking a degree in social work at university. I have absolutely loved my access course which has made me all the more eager to learn.

TIP!

Make sure your statement is all your own work. UCAS will use similarity detection software to check your statement against other statements. If they detect similarity they will inform the universities and colleges you've applied to. They'll also let you know. Each of your universities and colleges will decide independently what action to take.

24 | Adding a choice

This is one of the most important parts of your application – the outcome of all your research into higher education. It's often best to leave entering details of the courses you're applying to until you've completed all the factual information required and worked out your personal statement.

You're allowed a maximum of five course applications. You can apply to fewer than five if you want to, and can add further courses until the end of June as long as you haven't already accepted any offers. If you applied to only one course initially, you'll be allowed to add up to four additional choices, but only if you pay the difference between the single (£22.50) and multiple (£27) application fees – see Chapter 25 for more information on payments).

Add your university or college and your course

- Start typing the name of the university or college into the 'Institution' field – select from the options displayed.
- Do the same for the course you have selected.
- Locations and start dates are also displayed according to the course – you'll be able to choose the right ones for you.
- For most courses you'll leave 'Point of entry' blank – unless the university or college has agreed that you can join the second or third year of the course (more below).

See Figure 18, Add a course choice, opposite.

Start date

You can select from a list of available start dates. If you want to apply at this stage for deferred entry (that is, starting your course in 2024 rather than 2023), choose the correct date from the list. More information on deferred entry is given in Chapter 8. Your personal statement (see Chapter 23) gives you the chance to explain why you want to defer entry.

It's no use applying for 2024 entry if some of your exams won't be taken until 2024, as a final decision on this application has to be taken by September 2023 (unless otherwise agreed by the university or college).

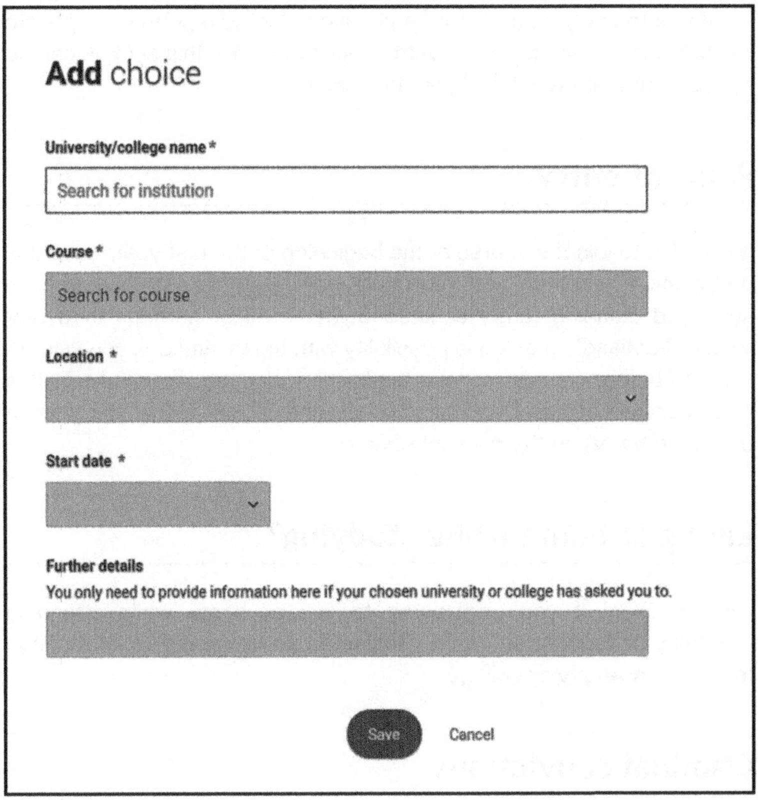

Figure 18: Add a course choice

Plus, you're not allowed to keep a deferred place at a university or college and then apply the following year to other institutions of the same kind. UCAS will intercept and cancel applications like these!

Further details

On many UCAS applications this part is left blank, but in some cases further information can be requested by universities or colleges. Check the UCAS search tool on www.ucas.com or the university or college prospectus to find out whether this is the case. The sort of information you may need to give could include:

- duration of the course (three- or four-year course)
- minor, subsidiary or first-year course option choice
- specialisations within your chosen course
- Qualified Teacher Status
- previous applications

- if you're applying to Oxford and have selected a permanent private hall (rather than a college with a campus code), this section can be used to state which hall you have chosen.

Point of entry

If you plan to join the course at the beginning of the first year, leave this part blank. If you think you may qualify for credit transfer or entry with advanced standing (entry at second-year level or perhaps third-year level in Scotland), check this possibility with the institutions you want to apply to before completing your application. You may then indicate this to the universities and colleges by entering '2' or '3' (i.e. the year of proposed entry) on the relevant course.

Living at home while studying?

Choose 'Yes' if you're planning to live at home while attending university or college, or 'No' if you'll need accommodation information from the university or college.

Criminal convictions

UCAS only asks applicants who apply for certain courses – for example, those that involve work with children and vulnerable adults – to declare whether they have any criminal convictions, including spent convictions. This question only appears if you are applying for one of these courses.

See Figure 19, Criminal convictions, opposite.

Certain professions or occupations are exempt from the Rehabilitation of Offenders Act (1974) or involve regulated activities – such as (but not limited to) teaching, medicine, dentistry, law, accountancy, actuarial, insolvency, healthcare, social work, veterinary medicine, veterinary science, pharmacy, osteopathy, chiropractic, optometry and professions or occupations involving work with children or vulnerable adults, including the elderly or sick people.

Different rules apply to such professions or occupations with regard to disclosure of information about criminal convictions. You may be required to disclose information regarding any convictions even if they are spent.

Some courses in respect of such professions or occupations involve an integral work placement and you may not be able to undertake such placement and complete your studies if you have criminal convictions.

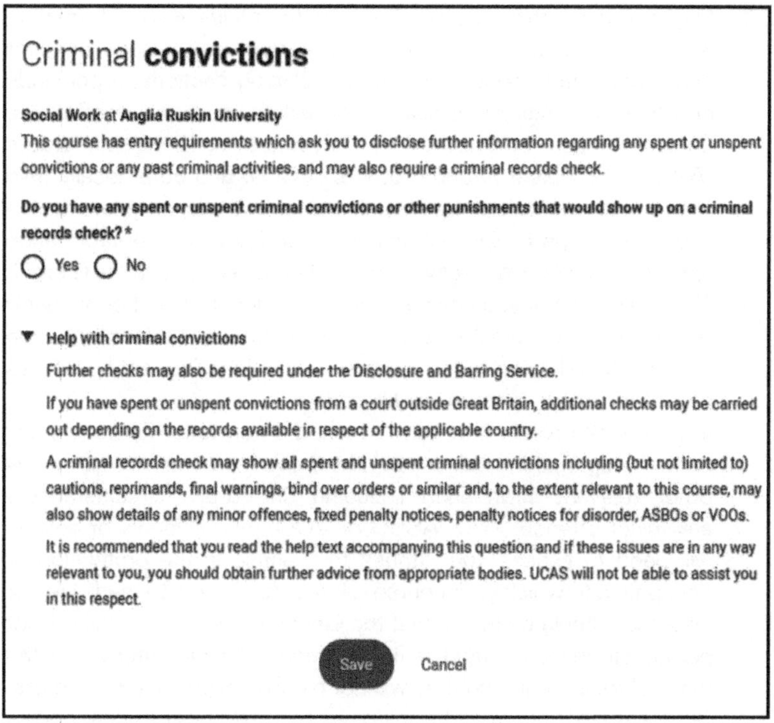

Criminal **convictions**

Social Work at **Anglia Ruskin University**

This course has entry requirements which ask you to disclose further information regarding any spent or unspent convictions or any past criminal activities, and may also require a criminal records check.

Do you have any spent or unspent criminal convictions or other punishments that would show up on a criminal records check? *

○ Yes   ○ No

▼ Help with criminal convictions

Further checks may also be required under the Disclosure and Barring Service.

If you have spent or unspent convictions from a court outside Great Britain, additional checks may be carried out depending on the records available in respect of the applicable country.

A criminal records check may show all spent and unspent criminal convictions including (but not limited to) cautions, reprimands, final warnings, bind over orders or similar and, to the extent relevant to this course, may also show details of any minor offences, fixed penalty notices, penalty notices for disorder, ASBOs or VOOs.

It is recommended that you read the help text accompanying this question and if these issues are in any way relevant to you, you should obtain further advice from appropriate bodies. UCAS will not be able to assist you in this respect.

Save   Cancel

Figure 19: Criminal convictions

Further, while you may be permitted to study for one of the above professions or occupations, you may not be able to register and practise upon completion of your course.

You should not declare convictions, cautions, warnings or reprimands which are deemed 'protected' under the Rehabilitation of Offenders Act 1974 (Exceptions) Order 1975 (as amended in 2013). A conviction or caution can become 'protected' as a result of a filtering process. Guidance and criteria on the filtering of convictions and cautions can be found on the Disclosure and Barring Service (DBS) website. Further information on filtering can be found at: www.gov.uk/government/collections/dbs-filtering-guidance.

You should be aware that in respect of these courses:

1. The university or college may ask you to provide further information regarding any convictions (including spent convictions), and/or may ask you to agree to a Disclosure and Barring Service (DBS) check.
2. Where required, the university or college will send you instructions regarding how to provide the information they require. They may send you documents to fill in. Where such documents come from will depend on the location of the college or university that you are applying to. Please see the table on page 165 for further information.

3. Depending on the type of check, different levels of information will be revealed. The information revealed may include unspent convictions and spent convictions (including cautions, reprimands and final warnings or similar). Information about minor offences, penalty notices for disorder (PNDs), anti-social behaviour orders (ASBOs) or violent offender orders (VOOs) and other locally held police information may be revealed where it is appropriate to the course for a particular occupation or profession. The information may be disclosed irrespective of when it occurred (unless it is filtered).

4. This means that if you have a criminal conviction (spent or unspent) or, in certain circumstances, any minor offence, this information may be made known to the university or college (but not UCAS) as part of the check (unless it is filtered).

5. If the check reveals that you have had a conviction (including any caution, reprimand, final warning, bind over order or similar) or any other relevant information including (in certain circumstances) any minor offence, PND, ASBO or VOO, the university or college will need to assess your fitness to practise in the profession or occupation to which your course relates. Applicants to medicine, for instance, should be aware that the General Medical Council will not permit students deemed unfit to practise to be entered on the medical register and so they will not be able to practise as doctors. Similar restrictions may be imposed by other professional bodies including (but not limited to) those connected with law, teaching, accountancy, social work, healthcare, veterinary services, pharmacy, financial and insurance services and the armed forces.

6. You may also be subject to further checks (before and/or after you complete your course) by prospective employers who will make their own assessments regarding your fitness to practise in the relevant profession or undertake the relevant occupation.

7. If these issues are in any way relevant to you, you should obtain further advice from appropriate bodies.

8. In England and Wales you may also be required to complete documentation and maintain a registration with the Disclosure and Barring Service (DBS). The DBS scheme is designed to allow universities and colleges to identify any individual who is barred from working with children and vulnerable adults, including elderly or sick people.

How will the university or college handle my application if I declare a criminal conviction?

If you tick the box you will not be automatically excluded from the application process. The information concerning criminal convictions will be passed to appointed persons at the university or college. In line with best admissions practice, they will consider your application separately from your academic and achievement merits. During this consideration, they may ask you to provide further information about your conviction. If they are satisfied, your application will proceed in the normal way although they may add certain conditions to any offer they may make. Otherwise, they won't notify you of their decision.

It's important to note that a failure to declare a criminal conviction is taken very seriously, and could result in expulsion from your university or college. You should therefore seek advice before answering this question if you are unsure how to answer it.

All information concerning criminal convictions must be treated sensitively, confidentially and managed in accordance with data protection legislation.

You may find further details about how a criminal conviction declaration is handled (including the right to appeal a decision) on the university or college website.

In addition, you may also find the details in the following table useful.

Region	Agency	Website address
England and Wales	Disclosure and Barring Service (DBS)	www.gov.uk/government/organisations/disclosure-and-barring-service
Scotland	Disclosure Scotland	www.disclosurescotland.co.uk
Northern Ireland	Access Northern Ireland	www.nidirect.gov.uk/accessni

You'll be asked this question each time you add a course that requires an enhanced criminal conviction declaration.

Once all choices are added select confirm choices

There's a maximum of five choices and choice restrictions still apply (a maximum of four courses in any one of medicine, dentistry, veterinary medicine or veterinary science).

TIP!

Don't forget that you can make insurance subject choices as alternatives to your applications to medicine, dentistry or veterinary medicine or science (see Chapter 8).

Admissions tests and assessments

Some courses have extra admissions tests and assessments which are further conditions you need to meet to confirm your place. You'll be able to read about these when researching your courses.

Find out more about admissions tests and assessments in Chapter 9.

Clicking the three dots at the bottom right of a card enables you to see a summary of the details. Any choice combinations that aren't permitted will be flagged with red text on the right of each relevant card.

See Figure 20, Admissions tests and assessment details, below.

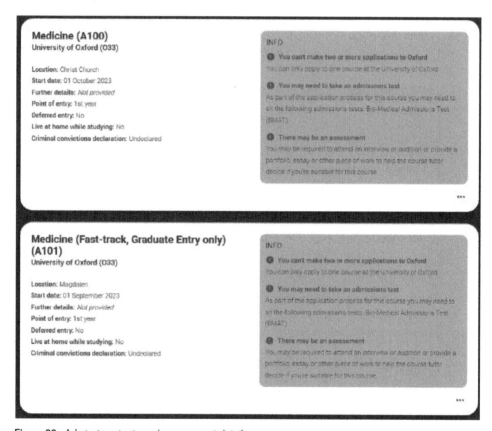

Figure 20: Admissions tests and assessment details

25 | Finishing your application

There are four steps to the submission process.

The application must be complete (showing 100%) before pressing submit.

See Figure 21, Application status, below.

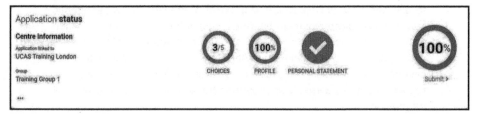

Figure 21: Application status

Declaration

Once you've completed all the sections, press 'Submit' and you'll be asked to read the declaration carefully, and only agree if you're absolutely sure that you're happy with its contents. UCAS can't process your application unless you confirm your agreement (with its terms and conditions), which legally binds you to make the required payment (see page 168).

When you submit your application, click 'Accept and proceed'.

Remember, by agreeing you're saying that the information you've provided is accurate, complete and all your own work and that you agree to abide by the rules of UCAS. You're also agreeing to your personal data being processed by UCAS and universities and colleges under the relevant data protection legislation. Any offer of a place you may receive is made on the understanding that, in accepting it, you also agree to abide by the rules and regulations of the institution.

To prevent and detect fraud of any nature, UCAS may have to give information about you to other organisations, including the police, the

Home Office, the Foreign and Commonwealth Office, UK Visas and Immigration, the Student Loans Company, local authorities, the SAAS, examination boards or awarding bodies, the Department for Work and Pensions and its agencies, and other international admissions organisations.

If UCAS or an institution has reason to believe that you or any other person has omitted any mandatory information requested in the instructions on the application, has failed to include any additional material information, has made any misrepresentation or given false information, UCAS and/or the institution will take whatever steps it considers necessary to establish whether the information given in your application is correct.

UCAS and the institutions reserve the right at any time to request that you, your referee or your employer provide further information relating to any part of your application, e.g. proof of identity, status, academic qualifications or employment history. If such information is not provided within the time limit set by UCAS, UCAS reserves the right to cancel your application. Fees paid to UCAS in respect of applications that are cancelled as a result of failure to provide additional information as requested, or as a result of providing fraudulent information, are not refundable.

False information is defined as including any inaccurate or omitted examination results. Omission of material information will include failure to complete correctly the declaration on the application relating to criminal convictions and failure to declare any other information that might be significant to your ability to commence or complete a course of study.

Submitting your application

Once you've agreed to the terms of the declaration, you can pass your application on to your UCAS coordinator or administrator – usually a head of sixth form, form teacher or careers adviser.

They'll check it over, add your written reference (see page 110), make arrangements for collecting your application fee and, finally, send it to UCAS.

If you find that you need to alter your application after you've submitted it, you should ask your UCAS coordinator or administrator to return it to you. You'll then be able to make the necessary changes before resubmitting it. If mistakes are spotted by the coordinator or administrator, they'll return it to you for amendments.

Payment

Application to higher education via UCAS costs £27 (or £22.50 if you apply to only one course).

Applying through your school or college

They'll let you know how they handle payments. Normally you'll pay by debit or credit card, but some schools and colleges prefer to collect applicant fees themselves and send UCAS a single payment covering everyone.

Applying as an individual

If you aren't making your application through a school or college, you'll need to make your payment online using a credit or debit card.

You don't need to make your payment until you've completed your application. Once you've agreed to the terms of use of the UCAS application in the declaration, you will be asked for your card details (if you're paying by this method). Apply will automatically know whether you should pay the full £27 or the single-choice fee of £22.50. UCAS accepts UK and international Visa, Visa Electron, Delta, MasterCard, JCB and Maestro credit and debit cards. At the moment it does not accept American Express or Diners Club cards. The card you use to pay doesn't need to be in your own name, but of course you'll require the consent of the cardholder.

What happens next?

On receipt of your application, UCAS will (usually within 48 hours) send out a welcome email containing your Personal ID and a copy of the list of your higher education course choices in random order. You should check this thoroughly and contact UCAS immediately if anything is incorrect.

You can log in to your application to follow its progress. Later in the application cycle you'll receive instructions from UCAS to help you conclude a successful higher education application. For more information on this and on offers, see Part II of this book.

26 | Troubleshooting

Some common problems

I can't log in ...

If your buzzword or password does not work, check the following.

- Have you entered the password correctly? Login details are case sensitive, so check that you have all the characters exactly right.
- Are you in the student area (not the staff area)?
- Is your computer properly connected to the internet?
- Are you able to connect to other websites?

If the answer to all of these questions is 'Yes', you may have a problem with your network or internet service provider. Try connecting to the main UCAS site, www.ucas.com – if you can, there may be a problem with the application system and you should call UCAS' Customer Experience Centre on 0371 4680 468.

I've forgotten my password ...

If you forget your password, click on 'Forgot your password' and enter the email address you provided on your application. UCAS will send you a reminder of your username and a link to reset your password.

Once you have successfully logged in, you can change your password.

> **TIP!**
>
> If you leave your UCAS application open without touching it, it will time out for security reasons and you'll have to log in again.

I've pasted my statement into my application and it's all gone wrong ...

The default character size for statements in your UCAS application is 12 point. If you've written your personal statement in Word and used a larger font size, it might not fit when you try to paste it into your application.

You may lose formatting when you paste your personal statement into your application – you should edit your statement very carefully. You won't be able to use bold or italicised fonts. Plus the character and line count may be different from those in your word-processing package. This is because formatting characters, such as paragraphs, are counted in the application but may not be counted in Word or Pages.

Need help?

Once you start completing your application, you can find help on each screen of your application. Most difficulties can be sorted out quickly by clicking on the question mark icon and following the instructions.

And finally ...

If you'd like more information on the application process, find out more at ucas.com.

If you decide to go ahead with your application, good luck! And get in touch with UCAS if you have any questions.

Glossary

BMAT
A test used by some universities in selecting applicants for medicine, but more widely used for entry to veterinary medicine and biomedical degree courses.

Careerscape
A website that can help students to choose higher education courses and careers: www.cascaid.co.uk.

Clearing
A service run by UCAS in the summer after all the advanced results are known, to match applicants without places with universities and colleges that still have vacant places.

Clearing Plus
An additional tool designed to help you find your perfect course. To speed things up, UCAS takes what they know about you, and what they know about the types of students unis are looking for, to suggest some courses you might like. You can express interest in courses, and the university or college can contact you.

CV
Curriculum vitae: a document detailing your qualifications and experience.

eCLIPS
Careers information online: www.eclips-online.co.uk. A licence is required to use this site.

Extra
A chance to make further applications in the spring for applicants who don't get any offers of places or don't accept any offers from their initial applications.

Higher Ideas
An online tool to help students to decide on suitable higher education courses: www.careersoft.co.uk/Products/Higher_Ideas.

Job Explorer Database
Careers information online: www.careersoft.co.uk/Products/Job_Explorer_Database.

LNAT
A test used by some universities in selecting applicants for law.

Morrisby Profile

An online careers assessment that gives job recommendations and also A level and higher education suggestions: www.morrisby.com/morrisby-profile.

MyUniChoices

An interactive program that gives higher education course and institution recommendations based on answers to preference-based questions: www.myunichoices.com.

Postgraduate

Someone studying on an advanced degree course, e.g. an MA or MSc.

Sandwich course

A degree or diploma course that includes work experience.

Seminar

A discussion in a small group of students, often, but not always, following a lecture on the same topic.

Tariff

The UCAS Tariff is used to allocate points to Level 3 qualifications, such as A levels, Highers, BTEC qualifications and others, making it easier for universities and colleges to compare applicants. Universities and colleges may use it when making offers to applicants.

T Levels

A new group of vocational qualifications equivalent to three A levels, introduced in September 2020.

Turing Scheme

The Turing scheme is a global study and work abroad programme, which replaced Erasmus+ from September 2021.

Tutorial

A discussion between a much smaller group of students than in a seminar (sometimes just one student) and a lecturer.

UCAS Hub

A personalised online space students can register for to explore post-18 options.

UCAT

A test used by some universities in selecting applicants for medicine.

Undergraduate

A student on a first degree course, e.g. BA, BSc.

Appendix: A note for staff on becoming a UCAS centre

Schools, educational advisers, and agents who assist students with UCAS Undergraduate applications to UK higher education can register to become a UCAS centre. It's completely free and means students can make their UCAS Undergraduate applications through you.

Not only will you be provided with a suite of tools to help manage your students' applications, you'll have access to the latest information and advice services, covering everything you need to know to support them through the application process.

To find out more about becoming a UCAS centre, visit ucas.com/becomeacentre.

Notes for UCAS centres

UCAS centres use the adviser portal, which gives a complete oversight of your students' applications and access to real-time data in one system. More information can be found at ucas.com/advisers.

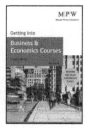